D0031633

BEARING WITNESS TO THE TRUTH

BETHEL SEMINARY WEST
LIBRARY
6116 Arosa Street
San Diego, CA 92115-3902

BEARING WITNESS TO THE TRUTH

HAROLD COOKE PHILLIPS

ABINGDON-COKESBURY PRESS
New York • *Nashville*

BEARING WITNESS TO THE TRUTH

COPYRIGHT MCMXLIX
BY PIERCE & SMITH

All rights in this book are reserved. No part of the
text may be reproduced in any form without written per-
mission of the publishers, except brief quotations used
in connection with reviews in magazines or newspapers.

Scripture quotations designated "A.S.V." are from the
American Standard Version of the Bible, copyright renewal,
1929, the International Council of Religious Education.
Those designated "Moffatt" are from *The Bible: A New
Translation,* by James Moffatt, copyright 1922, 1924, 1926,
1935 by Harper & Brothers.

SET UP, PRINTED, AND BOUND BY THE
PARTHENON PRESS, AT NASHVILLE,
TENNESSEE, UNITED STATES OF AMERICA

To
the members and friends of the
First Baptist Church, Cleveland, Ohio
with gratitude and affection

PREFACE

IN writing upon such a subject as truth one feels like a very small creature splashing about in a vast and boundless sea —a condition which obviously has its perils! As far as the Lyman Beecher lectureship is concerned, however, one would not need a large subject to induce the feeling of inadequacy. As he contemplates the giants of other generations, not to mention his own, who have stood in this succession, he realizes that the spies whom the Israelites sent on a reconnoitering mission to Canaan were not dealing in hyperbole when they said that the Canaanites were men of such stature that in comparison the Israelites seemed like grasshoppers. Such is my reaction. Of course there is this to be said on the other side: that since the majority of the ministers who may read this book will be in stature more like the Israelites than the Canaanites, it may not be a wholly unwise policy to give them some representation on the lectureship by occasionally choosing a lecturer from their number.

The book is a revision of the lectures, although they are being printed substantially as they were delivered. In revising them I have made them somewhat longer. This means that the patience of the reader will be taxed a little more than was that of the hearer, but then the reader has a much easier way of escape.

It is impossible of course for one adequately to express his indebtedness to others, even though he is happy to acknowledge it. In addition to those who have helped me through their writings I am deeply grateful to Professor Albert Suthers, head of the department of the history of religion at Ohio Wesleyan University, who graciously read the entire manuscript and made valuable suggestions. Nor could I forget my secretary, Miss Gladys Dray, who as usual has given efficient and tireless service.

The actual delivery of the lectures will long remain a most pleasant memory. The kindness of the faculty, to say nothing of the understanding spirit of the audience, gave me a big lift. I should like to express to Dean Luther A. Weigle my appreciation of his gracious hospitality, and to assure him and the other members of the faculty of the Yale Divinity School of my lasting gratitude.

HAROLD COOKE PHILLIPS

CONTENTS

I

WHAT IS TRUTH?

IN hardly any subject do we as ministers have more at stake than in the subject of truth. We are ambassadors of one described by the psalmist as the "God of truth" (31:5), who desires "truth in the inward parts" (51:6). This God, as we believe, has revealed himself most fully in him who said, "I am . . . the truth" (John 14:6). Jesus, moreover, spoke of "the Spirit of truth," who would "guide you into all the truth" (John 16:13). Christ's revelation reached its sublime heights on the cross, which, as Christians, we regard as the symbol of life's profoundest truth, "the power of God, and the wisdom of God" (I Cor. 1:24). It was as he faced his cross that Jesus spoke the words which form the title of this book. Said he to Pilate: "To this end was I born, and for this cause came I into the world, that I should BEAR WITNESS UNTO THE TRUTH. . . . Pilate saith unto him, What is truth?" (John 18:37-38.)

Whether or not these words be the *ipsissima verba* of Jesus is neither here nor there. They may be considered his *ipsissima vita*, his very life. We may doubt if he ever voiced them; we cannot doubt that he lived them. He did more than make them vocal—he made them vital.[1] The truth of these words is beyond the reach of textual criticism. They are verified in the larger context of life itself, and the testimony of life convinces as the language of the lips never does. "What is truth?" asks Pilate. The Christian answer is not a definition but a revelation, a life that lived the truth, revealed the truth, and spent itself in bearing witness to the truth.

To say this is not to say that there are not numerous definitions of truth. Perhaps as familiar and adequate a one as any would be that truth is the correspondence between our thoughts and reality, as truthfulness is the correspondence between our words and our thoughts. No definition of truth, however, is wholly satisfactory. For truth is an ultimate, and it is never possible adequately to define an ultimate. Let us therefore seek to answer the question "What is truth?" not by defining it but by describing it. Of course in no sense will the description be exhaustive. It will not be exhaustive if for no other reason than that we shall discuss the subject primarily within the framework of the Christian faith.

This does not mean that the discussion may not at times have a slightly philosophic flavor, for there will be reference to philosophers and even appraisal of some philosophic theories—but solely because such philosophic excursions are essential to the development of the theme. Our primary interest is not philosophic but religious.[2] This is not to imply any antithesis

---

[1] This observation may apply to the many other references to John's Gospel throughout these chapters.

[2] The more general word "religious" is used rather than "Christian," though, as will be evident, it is the Christian faith to which these chapters point.

12

between philosophy and religion, between speculation and experience. For philosophy is the handmaid of theology—*ancilla theologiae*, as the schoolmen described it. To a degree they will ever be kin and complementary. It is true that the God of philosophy has not always been the God of Abraham, Isaac, and Jacob; yet it is also true that often the highest type of philosophic thinking has been done by theologians. We should not forget that some of the great names in the field of philosophy have held first rank in the councils of the church.

To a certain extent this is so even in our own day. I am thinking now of men like Reinhold Niebuhr and the late Archbishop of Canterbury, William Temple, to name but two. It was the latter who, in commenting on the assertion that philosophy by and large tends to be antitheistic, wrote: "But in fact the weight of the general philosophic argument tells, in my judgment, decisively the other way." [3] The point is, however, that truth for the philosopher moves in the realm of abstract theories and metaphysical propositions, while for the minister it is related to life in its vast and complex situations. The God of the Bible has nothing in common with Aristotle's "detached and self-sufficient Prime Mover." [4] All through the Judaic-Christian tradition truth is involved in the most practical concerns of men as they face life situations. For this reason the Christian minister has much more at stake in the cause of truth than does the philosopher. For to the minister truth is not just an academic football to be kicked about on

[3] *Christ the Truth*, p. 46.
[4] George F. Thomas, *Central Christian Affirmations*. See also *The Christian Answer*, ed. Henry P. Van Dusen, p. 103.

playing fields of such elevation that the air is too rarefied for any but the acclimated to breathe, and the rules of the game so highly technical and involved that only the professionally trained may participate; rather, truth is related to the whole business of living. Philosophy's concern for truth grows primarily out of its interest in knowledge. Religion's concern for truth grows primarily out of its interest in the abundant life, which, while it includes knowledge, embraces a great deal else besides.

It will be evident from this that we are thinking of truth in terms of the sum total of reality.[5] There is of course another way of considering it. If we say, "The sun is shining," and it does happen to be shining, we are saying that which is true— we are stating a fact which can be verified by knowledge. Truth, however, is vastly bigger and more significant than events or data amenable to factual verification. We must distinguish between what is true, and what is truth; between truths and the truth. We shall be thinking of truth as a synonym for reality, a way of describing the very stuff of the universe.

With this preliminary statement let us proceed now to consider what, from the viewpoint of the Christian faith, are some of the characteristic marks of truth. There are three primary characteristics. I venture to call them axioms. Each axiom has its corollary, so that we shall have three pairs of observations concerning truth.

The first observation is that truth is objectively real, in the

[5] In *Living Issues of Philosophy* Professor Titus defines reality as "the state or quality of being real or actually existent, in contrast to what is mere appearance." (P. 269.)

sense of being veritable; it has "being." It is not gross, subject to weight, conformable to shape, and yet it may be amenable to sense perception. Through sense it may manifest itself, and by the senses it may be interpreted. Indeed, truth often comes to us embodied; it may itself be invisible, but its presence, its nature, may be sensed and felt. If it were not so there would be nothing to save us mortals from being plunged into the chaos and confusion of moral relativism, if not complete nihilism. "It was natural that in the practice of the Eddy philosophy and theology a great deal of obvious bunkum should creep into the system, for when all objective reality is denied, what then is truth?" [6] Our gospel insists therefore that truth is objectively real. "O send out thy light and thy truth: let them lead me." (Ps. 43:3.) "The law was given through Moses; grace and truth came through Jesus Christ." (John 1:17. A.S.V.) "The truth is not with the right, nor with the left, nor in the middle, but in the heights." [7]

To say that truth is objectively real is to say that man never creates it but only discovers it. It is a fact worth pondering that the forces organically related to this universe, whether physical or moral, are wholly beyond the reach of man either to create or to destroy. This of itself should be an unfailing source of strength to the minister. For in so far as he preaches the truth he is not just voicing his opinions or prating ideas which are subjectively real to him but may not be real at all; he is on the contrary dealing with what is as realistic as the pulpit, the pews, or the people who sit in them. Indeed, more so, because

[6] E. F. Dakin, *Mrs. Eddy*, p. 221.
[7] Quoted by P. T. Forsyth, *Positive Preaching and the Modern Mind*, p. 888.

They shall perish, but thou shalt endure;
Yea, all of them shall wax old like a garment;
As a vesture shalt thou change them, and they shall be changed:
But thou art the same,
And thy years shall have no end. (Ps. 102:26-27.)

His truth endureth to all generations. (Ps. 100:5.)

Paul, in writing to the Corinthians, warned about the trumpet giving an uncertain sound (I Cor. 14:8). He was referring particularly to those who were speaking in tongues and hence unintelligible. Our uncertainty does not make us unintelligible but unconvincing. Someone has remarked that whereas the minister of another generation would pound the desk and say, "Thus saith the Lord," the modern minister is more likely to observe, "I see where Mr. So-and-So says." Now it is unquestionably true that a minister's "Thus saith the Lord" is sometimes more an expression of his own limitations than a revelation of the divine wisdom or will. He is in constant danger of identifying his prejudices, self-interests, ecclesiastical arrogance, or pride with the truth. This is unfortunate. The fact is, however, that the truth he is set to proclaim is not his truth nor that of those to whom he speaks. It is the truth about man, but it is not man's truth. From the Christian point of view we could say of truth what John said of those who believed, who "were born, not of blood, nor of the will of the flesh, nor of the will of man, but of God" (John 1:13).

A suggestion comes to us from the language of science as to the nature of truth. We speak of "Euclid's theorem," of "Boyle's law," or of "Einstein's theory" in such fashion that one

WHAT IS TRUTH

might think these men created such realities. Actually, however, the theorem, law, or theory, in so far as it is true, is simply a description of the way nature works. Man masters nature only as he obeys her. He gets nature to do his will only as he bends his will to hers. As Bacon put it: "Nature can only be controlled by being obeyed." The door to scientific truth can never be forced by arrogant or self-assertive hands, yet it yields readily to the touch of him who co-operates with nature by obeying her laws, which, we repeat, man discovers but never creates.

This is not in any way to belittle the role of the discoverer. As has been said: "If the earth surrendered to the sun, the whole solar system surrendered to Copernicus." [8] In a real sense the discoverer is more significant than the law he discovers, since it is the discoverer who makes actual what, until he appeared, was only potential. This fact, however, does not in any sense affect the objective nature of scientific truth. In a conversation with the Indian mystic Sir Rabindranath Tagore, Albert Einstein is reported to have said:

I cannot prove that scientific truth must be conceived as a truth that is valid independent of humanity; but I believe it firmly. . . . We attribute to truth a superhuman objectivity; it is indispensable to us, this reality that is independent of our existence and our experience and our mind, though we cannot say what it means.[9]

This observation holds good not only for scientific truth but for all truth. It certainly holds good for moral and spiritual

[8] Lynn Harold Hough, *Personality and Science*, p. 22.
[9] George Seldes, *Freedom of the Press*, p. xv.

17

truth. Suppose, for example, we should decide to abolish the moral law as expressed in the Ten Commandments. After all, the Ten Commandments have been around for a long time. Let someone move therefore that they be abolished. The motion is seconded and carried. Now actually what should we have done? Nothing at all! For it is quite beyond the ability of man to abolish the Ten Commandments. They are in very truth imbedded in the moral structure of the universe. Written on stone—how could their enduring nature be better symbolized? Wholly to disregard them would be to destroy the very foundation of our civilization. A state may pass a law to make gambling legal and the Roman Catholic Church may give it a place of good and regular standing in ecclesiastical practice, but that does not make gambling right nor alter in the slightest degree its deteriorating effect on character. We can repeal prohibition—I am not saying that under the circumstances we should not have done so—but we cannot repeal the effect which the immoderate use of alcohol has on the human system; that is written in body tissue, nerve ganglia, and brain cells. The plain fact is that when it comes to moral reality, majority votes mean nothing whatsoever. Questions of right and wrong, truth and error, are not settled by a show of hands. This lies beyond the whims, passions, and prejudices of man. "The larger the crowd, the more probable that that which it praises is folly, and the more improbable that it is truth." [10] Truth is not made more true when the majority shout its praises, nor less true when they shout "Crucify!" and send it

[10] Sören Kierkegaard, *Purity of Heart*, p. 175.

to a cross. We all want "the right of private judgment," but we need constantly to remember that our private judgments are not always right, and must at last bow to the superior judgment of truth which is objectively there.

In this connection one cannot but point out what seems to be a serious error in the philosophy of pragmatism. This philosophy, usually connected with the name of William James, is considered as distinctly American as Thanksgiving turkey or wieners and buns. Professor James, however, referred to it as "a new name for old ways of thinking." It probably springs from the teachings of Kant, who started other ideas besides the philosophy of pragmatism. With the more up-to-date or "left-wing pragmatism"—instrumentalism—the name of John Dewey is connected.

There is just one aspect of the philosophy of pragmatism which now concerns us, namely, its view of truth. Pragmatism does not admit that there is any such thing as objective truth, nor a disinterested view of truth. The pragmatist does not say that through experiment one discovers truth; he says that through experiment one makes truth, creates it. In Professor James's words: "Truth *happens* to an idea. It *becomes* true, is *made* true by events. Its verity *is* in fact an event, a process: the process namely of its verifying itself, its veri-*fication*." [11] Plainly, according to this philosophy, truth is not that which we discover or which is there to be discovered; we do not find truth, we make truth. That is to say, we make reality. But as William P. Montague says: "Truth is never created; it is found, partly by the senses, partly by the intellect." He

[11] *Pragmatism*, p. 201.

19

says further: "A proposition that was not true before it was discovered could never become true by being discovered."[12]

As opposed to pragmatism we may view man's relation to truth as objective reality somewhat as follows: Four steps are involved. First is the belief that truth is objective. Second, one becomes aware of this truth, experiences it. Third, one gives expression to his experience, makes it articulate. The fourth and final step is that such living testimony will like a guide-post point the way to the reality through contact with which other seekers may find the truth.[13]

Apply this process to the Christian's faith in God. First is the belief that God is objectively real. Second, one has an experience of God, comes to know him. God speaks to him as to Moses through the burning bush, or as to Hosea through a poignant domestic tragedy, or as to Isaiah in some exalted moment of worship, or as to Amos in the call of righteousness or justice. Third, such souls give expression to these experiences verbally or in writing; and then finally you and I, who read their testimony, try to get back to the objective reality whence the faith originated, and so have a firsthand experience our-selves. Our constant danger of course is that we shall fail to do this. We take the formula, the doctrine, the statement of another's faith—the "Jesus whom Paul preacheth" (Acts 19: 13)—repeat it parrot fashion, and in so doing miss the truth. For truth becomes truth for us only when we go behind the formula by which it is expressed to the objective reality which

[12] *Ways of Knowing,* p. 125.

[13] A much more adequate description of these steps will be found in Hazen Miller's *Christian Truth in History,* pp. 109 ff.

is expressed. The truth is not the formula but what produced the formula. "God is love" is not truth for me until I come "to know the love of Christ which passeth knowledge" (Eph. 3:19).

Now if truth is objectively real, it follows as a sort of corollary that it is the basic ingredient in every relationship of life—indeed, it is the keystone in the arch of life itself. As Edgar Sheffield Brightman says: "The ideal of truth underlies and grounds all other ideals: for if any pretended ideal is not true—that is, not a true ideal—how can it pretend to be anything more than a false opinion about an ideal?" [14] Truth is therefore life's supreme priority. Since we cannot create it, our primary business is to try to discover it, come to terms with it, and adjust ourselves to it.

As one understands this fundamental nature of truth and the need of man to come to terms with it, he becomes increasingly concerned about those forces in our society that practice and propagate deception. Not the least evil of war is that it trains a generation in the art of deception. The science of camouflage plays a major and sometimes decisive role. To mislead or deceive the enemy is our constant aim. Sometimes sincere speeches are made by responsible men with the sole intention of misleading the enemy. But the enemy is not the only one who is harmed. Our aim of course is to demoralize the enemy while we build our morale. But such an end is ultimately impossible in a moral universe. As it works out, the deceiver as well as the deceived is affected by the *ruses de guerre*.

[14] "The Church, the Truth, and Society," in *Theology and Modern Life,* ed. Paul Arthur Schilpp, p. 256.

One might refer here to the psychological and moral havoc wrought in European Christians by being obliged to lie to the enemy occupying power in order to escape cruel death themselves or to defend their loved ones, and who, now that the crisis is past and the war over, find it difficult to recover their sense of moral values or adhere to their former standards.

In times of peace we by no means escape the flood of misrepresentation and deception. Much of modern commercial advertising sees to that. None of us can estimate the effect on the mind and spirit of an age submitted, as is ours, to the "advertising racket." The stream of high-pressure advertising, with its exaggerated and often baseless claims, does something sinister to us. An age constantly exposed to such an endless torrent of misrepresentation and deception—to "the loud pushfulness of blatant advertisements about little nothings" [15] —is in danger of losing its capacity for recognizing or even believing in truth. Paul might have been writing not to the Thessalonians but to the Americans when he pointed out that to those who "received not the love of the truth" God sends "delusion, that they should believe a lie." (II Thess. 2:10-11.)

Herbert Agar aptly describes our situation when he says: "Nobody believes the nonsense in any one advertisement." And yet, he continues: "Everyone is affected by the mist of deception which we continually breathe." [16] And Dorothy Thompson has remarked: "As a youngster fed on candy bars loses the taste for bread and butter, so a nation fed on false

[15] Arthur John Gossip, *In the Secret Place of the Most High*, p. 16.
[16] *A Time for Greatness*, p. 156.

values loses touch with truth and reality." [17] Indeed, as one contemplates the insincerity and distortion that undergird and permeate so much of our modern life, he is reminded of the story of the small boy who was once asked to define an abstract noun. He replied: "An abstract noun is the name of something that does not exist, like truth and honesty." However, any system, political, economic, or social, that is built on deception or dishonesty, like the house built on the sand, is bound to fall. Truth is the indispensable ingredient in every relationship. It is not a "theoretical luxury" but a "moral necessity."

It is our failure to see this that accounts for most of the chaos and calamities that befall us. We do not live as though truth were an objective reality and hence indispensable, but as though it were a social custom, a convention or convenience, to be brushed aside should it get in our way, as it often does. It is amazing that an age that bows so obediently to indispensable natural law should adopt so naïve an attitude to the moral law. Listen to this from Nietzsche: "The falseness of an opinion is not for us any objection to it. The question is, how far an opinion is life-furthering, life-preserving, species-preserving, perhaps species-rearing." [18] One marvels at the seemingly complete lack of moral insight that lies behind such a statement, for how could a false idea ever be "life-furthering" or "life-preserving"? As if a corrupt tree could bring forth good fruit, or men could gather grapes of thorns or figs of thistles. It is this moral naïveté that lies behind most of our woes. We know that in the physical realm we reap what we sow, that we cannot

[17] *Cleveland Plain Dealer,* Dec. 3, 1947.
[18] William Ernest Hocking, *Types of Philosophy,* pp. 144-45.

put disease germs in the blood stream and expect them to be "life-furthering" or "life-preserving"; but we think we can build a civilization on trickery, force, or fraud and expect it to produce security and well-being.

Here again we must refer to William James. He has contributed so very much to our thinking that it would be most unfortunate should criticism of some aspects of his thought be regarded as a lack of appreciation of his significant and most valuable contributions. But I, for one, cannot agree with him when he writes: "The notion of a reality calling on us to 'agree' with it, and that for no reason, but simply because its claim is 'unconditional' or 'transcendent,' is one that I can make neither head nor tail of." [19] That way of putting the matter is not, as it seems to me, quite fair to reality. Reality does not ask us to "agree" with it because its claims are "unconditional" and "transcendent." At least that is not why we obey the laws of gravity or the laws of health. We do so because these laws are an organic part of the universe to which we are organically related, and because we have found it "life-furthering" and "life-preserving" to co-operate with such realities. We are born into a universe that is a going concern, and are suddenly thrust upon the playing field of life, but the game has been going on long before we came on the scene. In a moral sense our first duty is to learn the rules, not to make them.

If this seems naïve, then observe what happens when men try to make them. Benito Mussolini said that in working out his political policy he owed much to Nietzsche and William James. No doubt the dictator read into the latter's writings

[19] *Pragmatism*, pp. 234-35.

24

implications that were never intended. Still, these were the men who, Mussolini said, "led him to discard 'pure reason' or 'a priori principles,' and to adopt those policies which work out best in practice." Said he: "The true policies are the expedient policies." [20] How expedient, one may add, he and his empire, so quickly turned to dust, will testify. Those too were Adolf Hitler's sentiments. The duty of the Germans, he once said, is "not to seek out objective truth in so far as it may be favorable to others, but uninterruptedly to serve one's own truth." [21] The fact that these two moral idiots were permitted to use the world as a huge guinea pig for carrying out their experiments of deceit and treachery is not simply a reflection on them but on the moral illiteracy of an age which does not seem aware of "the stern-eyed goddess of Truth." [22] How convincingly does history substantiate the observation of John Bennett, when he writes: "Nothing in all the world is more dangerous or more false than the situation where a thing comes to be regarded as true or right if only a dictator or minister of propaganda says it often enough." [23]

Not all the moral idiots, however, are across the seas. When Mussolini was riding high, thousands of American tourists came back from Italy singing his praises because he made the Italian trains run on time and provided hotels with American plumbing. These "innocents abroad," morally speaking, were wholly unconcerned about the moral incongruities of fascism.

[20] Hocking, *Types of Philosophy*, p. 144.
[21] Norman Angel, *Peace and the Plain man*, p. 62.
[22] Sir Charles Walston, *An Essay in Moral Reconstruction*, p. 28.
[23] *Christianity and Our World*, p. 54.

They did not realize that a system based upon tyranny, oppression, and expediency was doomed sooner or later to destruction. They did not understand that to gain an immediate advantage by betraying an ultimate truth was to strike a poor bargain. Our country is full of such citizens—men and women who do not seem to understand that "one's own truth" has to reckon with the objective realities of a moral universe which we shall have to learn to get along with, if we are going to get along at all, since truth is its indispensable ingredient. The morally obtuse are the greatest enemies of society, especially when they occupy places of power, as unfortunately for the world they so frequently do.

We come now to consider what, from a Christian point of view, may be regarded as a second axiom concerning truth: all truth is one. Nothing that is really true in one realm could possibly contradict what is really true of some other aspect of reality. "The music of the spheres" is no mere figure of speech. Truths never "collide." This is because we live in a universe expressive of the will of one God, whom we believe to be the creator and sustainer of all that is. To say that the truth concerning one aspect of reality is at daggers drawn with the truth of some other aspect would be to put civil strife at the very heart of God's creation. That is incredible! "If a kingdom be divided against itself, that kingdom cannot stand," said the Master (Mark 3:24)—an observation that is just as relevant to the kingdom of truth.

While, however, truth is one, there are different approaches to it. In the book of Revelation we are told that there are twelve gates to the city. So with the City of Truth we advance from different directions. Philosophy provided the first highway to the City of Truth, and for centuries was the only one. Philosophy conceives of truth as a series of logical propositions, and finds truth in "a set of mutually consistent ideas." The religious or, more specifically, theological approach held the field for some twelve centuries. While Christian theologians, many of whom were learned philosophers, did not discard the intellectual approach to truth nor deem the role of reason untrustworthy, still they tended to test the validity of a proposition "by its coherence with revealed truth, i.e., with dogmas." The most recent approach to truth is the scientific. It started about three hundred years ago. In this realm "the truth of a proposition is determined by its coherence with empirical data, . . . with things." [24]

Instead of thinking of truth approached by different roads, we might view it, as do some philosophers, as lying in different strata. Or again we may use Paul's figure of the body and its members. He was the first Christian thinker to discover, or at least to voice, the principle of unity in diversity—many members but one body. But in any event truth is one. If we accept the symbol of the roads, then we insist that when the travelers arrive at the truth they will all meet where the roads converge. If we prefer the symbol of different strata, then we must regard the strata as different floors of a building "fitly framed together" (Eph. 2:21), the whole structure a unit. Or if we prefer Paul's familiar symbol of the body and its members, then we must insist that though there be many members the body is one, not many.

[24] Harold Bosley, *The Quest for Religious Certainty*, pp. 12-14.

The failure to realize this has resulted in many unprofitable conflicts, like those between science and religion, for example. These conflicts mean one of two things—either that neither side has the truth, or, having the truth, one or both sides are trying to make it operative in an area of life over which it rightly has no authority. Well-meaning Christians, for instance, have tried to make the Bible an authority in science; and dogmatic scientists—the woods are full of them—have insisted that since the highly specialized techniques of the scientific laboratory are unavailable in dealing with the imponderables, therefore the great insights and values of our religion are fairy tales. It is at least comforting to realize that not all the fundamentalists are in the field of religion. In the field of science, however, there is less excuse for them, since a narrow-minded, arrogant, scientific dogmatist is a most unscientific phenomenon, and betrays the basic principle of science itself, which is an open-minded and unprejudiced approach to reality. The fact is that in the field of truth "the eye cannot say unto the hand, I have no need of thee: nor again, the head to the feet, I have no need of you." (I Cor. 12:21.)

Indeed we might go further and say that not only is all truth one, but that goodness, truth, and beauty, the classical trilogy by which the Greeks sought to express reality, are one also. Goodness, truth, and beauty are not three different values but one absolute value expressing itself in three forms: the moral, the intellectual, the aesthetic. I hope I shall not seem to be reading into Jesus' sayings that which is not there, but three sayings or incidents in the life of the Master would seem to substantiate this suggestion. There are many ways in

28

which he taught that men might find God. He spoke of seeing God, the ultimate Reality, in the face of a child; so character, goodness, was a symbol of the Eternal. He said people could read the heavens but could not discern the signs of the times—shall we say, were insensible to the truth, the imponderables that go to make up moral reality? Moreover he asked men to consider the lilies of the field and in their beauty to find God. So the face of a child, goodness; the signs of the times, truth; or the lilies of the field, beauty, were to Jesus symbols of the one Reality that lies back of all life—God. The poet's familiar couplet:

"Beauty is truth, truth beauty,"—that is all
Ye know on earth, and all ye need to know,[25]

is more than sentimental nonsense. Keat's insight is valid. So too was Wordsworth's when he defined poetry as "truth carried alive into the heart by passion."

Because truth is one it follows as a sort of corollary that truth is universal. Whatever is true anywhere is true everywhere. If two plus two make four in New Haven, they do not make five in Cairo or seven in Tokyo. The universality of scientific truth is generally recognized. The physical laws with which God undergirds his universe do not operate one way north of the equator and another way south of it, one way in the laboratory of an American college and another way in a college "down under" in Australia. Scientifically speaking what is true anywhere is true everywhere.

The same applies in the realm of art and aesthetics. Beauty

[25] John Keats, "Ode on a Grecian Urn."

is universal; it only waits upon the education of man's faculties to appreciate it. It speaks the common language of the human soul. There are English artists and French artists and German artists, but there is no such thing as English beauty or French beauty or German beauty, any more than there is American algebra or German geometry. Beauty is beauty whether one sees it in an English countryside, the Italian lake district, the Canadian Rockies, or the American Northwest. Beauty belongs to a frontierless kingdom. To walk through an art gallery is like stepping across national boundaries without ever once feeling that you are in a foreign land.

The same may be said of music. Once while listening to Brahms's *Second Symphony* over the radio I heard in one of its nuances the hum of an airplane winging its way overhead through the darkened sky. I thought, "Not only are the scientific laws that keep that plane in the sky universally valid, but the truth at the heart of this deeply moving symphony is universal too." All great music completely transcends every particularism of race or nationality. Elgar an Englishman, Beethoven a German, Sibelius a Finn, Grieg a Norwegian, MacDowell an American, Chopin a Frenchman, Tchaikovsky a Russian, Paderewski a Pole—to mention a few—all speak a universal language which utterly transcends the particularisms that separated them or us. Once a missionary played a recording of Handel's *Hallelujah Chorus*. The natives could not speak English, but as the strains rose from that magnificent production their eyes filled with tears. They felt the truth of its message.

Does not this hold good for moral truth also? Admittedly

moral standards vary, but do not moral laws work with surprising consistency in all ages and places? Is not Paul's statement "The wages of sin is death" (Rom. 6:23) just as true in twentieth-century America as it was in first-century Palestine? "Whatsoever a man soweth, that shall he also reap" (Gal. 6:7) is a principle from the ethical consequences of which the modern prodigal in the far country fares no better than the prodigal of song and story. By and large in any age or clime, revenge and cruelty are dragon's teeth that sprout a bitter harvest, while love begets love and kindness begets kindness. This is not to say that the moral laws of God can be validated as neatly and quickly as physical ones. "God is not like a hasty-tempered man, venting his anger at once on the occasion of every wrong." [26] But only those who are blind to the spiritual implications of history or cannot read the signs of the times will doubt the universal relevance of moral reality.

Can we now take a further step and suggest that not only scientific, aesthetic, and moral truth but religious truth, or more specifically Christian truth, is universal? This is our faith.

> In Christ there is no East or West,
> In him no South or North;
> But one great fellowship of love
> Throughout the whole wide earth.
>
> In him shall true hearts everywhere
> Their high communion find;
> His service is the golden cord
> Close binding all mankind. [27]

[26] Solon, Frag. 13, line 25.
[27] John Oxenham.

That there is in Christ that which appeals to man as man, regardless of race, class, or nation, is as well attested a fact of history and experience as any fact could be. That the truth in Christ completely transcends and renders relatively trivial all the exaggerated particularisms in which race, nationality, social standing, or culture involve us, is not a matter of argument—argument can be most inconclusive—but of experience and history.

This is not to say that universal truths are unknown in other religions outside Christianity. Some of the insights of Buddhism into reality are enduringly true. Gautama's ethic is regarded as one of the most original the world has ever known. Yet on the whole the faith misses validity and hence universality "because it does not exalt the good as an end in itself, but only as the means to the passive goal of nirvana." [28] In Judaism there are flashes of universalism. Amos asks: "Are ye not as the children of the Ethiopians unto me, O children of Israel? saith the Lord." (9:7.) Malachi asks: "Have we not all one father? hath not one God created us?" (2:10.) In Isaiah the universalistic note is even more evident: "Unto me every knee shall bow, every tongue shall swear." (45:23.) All genuine universalism in religion springs from monotheism. In theory therefore Judaism was universalistic. Actually, however, Judaism by and large was unable to transcend its racial and national prejudices. One reason for its determined opposition to Jesus was that he discarded its exclusiveness and embraced universality. This statement finds authoritative corroboration in the words of the cele-

[28] Louise Saxe Eby, *The Quest for Moral Law*, p. 48.

brated Jewish scholar Joseph Klausner, who, in speaking of the universal elements of Christianity, writes:

In the self-same moment he [Jesus] both annulled *Judaism* as the *life-force* of the Jewish nation, and also the nation itself as a nation. For a religion which possesses only a certain conception of God and a morality acceptable to *all* mankind, does not belong to any special nation, and, consciously or unconsciously, breaks down the barriers of nationality. This inevitably brought it to pass that his people, Israel, rejected him.[29]

The belief that the truth revealed in Jesus is intended for "all the world" and "every creature" undergirds our missionary endeavor. We send missionaries not because we think the other religions are wholly false, but because we believe they are only partly true, and that in Christ we have the truth.[30] If Jesus were only another wise teacher, and Christianity just another religion, Christian missions would be an impertinence. If, however, we believe that in Christ God has revealed his fullest and completest truth, that the universality of Christ grows out of his unique character, then Christian missions, far from being an impertinence, become an imperative—as great an imperative in the spiritual realm as scientific medicine or sanitation in the physical realm. Indeed many of us would say more so.

The need of our age for some universal truth in which the fragmentary, and hence disintegrating, aspects of our life can cohere is too obvious to be argued. Our age is in search

[29] *Jesus of Nazareth*, p. 390.
[30] This will be discussed more fully in the final chapter.

of universality. "It is done with individualism and the atomization of life into competitive and centrifugal elements." [31] The violent demonic totalitarian movements which have shaken our civilization to pieces give tragic proof of this. Communism, fascism, nazism, despite their differences, have this in common: they are attempts to pick up and tie together the scattered and hence disintegrating cultural interests of mankind.[32] This is why all of these "isms" are at heart religious. The tragedy of the totalitarian schemes, however, lies in this, that they are themselves but fragments. Both by word and deed they flatly and tragically deny their universalistic pretensions. They take race or class or state, inadequate concepts every one of them, and try to stretch them into all inclusiveness. It is the utter impossibility of any such undertaking that gives to these movements their demonic character and makes them the curse and crime that they are. They do reveal, however, man's deep hunger for some organizing center, some truth big enough in which his life and his culture can cohere and so find a meaning beyond themselves.

"Wilt thou be made whole?" asked the Master. (John 5:6.) Where else can we find wholeness save in the God whom Christ has revealed, the God and Father of our Lord Jesus Christ, who "made of one every nation of men to dwell on all the face of the earth"? (Acts 17:26 A.S.V.) "For he is our peace, who hath made both one, and hath broken down the middle wall of partition." (Eph. 2:14.) Countless multitudes

[31] Charles Clayton Morrison, *What Is Christianity?* p. 258.

[32] A fine analysis of this and other aspects of our culture will be found in Hugh Tigner's *Our Prodigal Son Culture.*

34

could testify with Paul that Christ has "slain the enmity" which separates them from their fellows, "for through him we both have access by one Spirit unto the Father" (Eph. 2:16, 18), the Father of all mankind. It is well-nigh tragic that so many professing Christians, while bearing witness to this blessed truth with their lips, deny it with their lives.

So far we have made two pairs of observations concerning truth. We have noted that truth is objectively real and hence indispensable. In the second place we have noted that all truth is one, and hence truth is universal. A third Christian axiom is that truth is indestructible, imperishable. "Opinions alter, manners change, creeds rise and fall, but the moral law is written on the tablets of eternity. . . . Justice and truth alone endure and live."[33] "The gates of hell shall not prevail against it." (Matt. 16:18.)

There are three reasons for our faith in the imperishable nature of truth and its ultimate triumph. For one thing time is on its side. Time is always on the side of the genuine. It is the counterfeit coin whose days are numbered. The coin that rings true stays in circulation. C. H. Spurgeon said: "A lie travels round the world while Truth is putting on her boots." Mark Twain observed that a lie is more of a sprinter than the truth. Granted. But given time, truth will overtake a lie and move ahead.

Illustrations of this will occur from all areas of life. Science offers many. Take but one. Ptolemy, the first astronomer of antiquity, taught in the second century that the earth was

[33] James Anthony Froude. Quoted by John Baillie, *What Is Christian Civilization?* p. 49.

the center of the universe. For generations everybody believed that it was and that the stars and planets revolved around it. But everybody was wrong. It took more than a thousand years to correct this error, but corrected it was. Copernicus, the founder of modern astronomy, thirteen centuries later hit upon the truth about our solar system and the Copernican astronomy replaced the Ptolemaic. Scientific hypotheses are always provisional. The mortality rate among such hypotheses is high indeed, but the hypothesis that is really true never dies. It wears well. Time is on its side.

In the field of the Christian religion numerous examples will come to mind. Time was, for instance, in the history of our religion when everyone believed that all suffering was due to sin. Bad people suffered because they were bad, but good people always had bright skies and clear sailing. That sin sometime, somehow, always results in suffering is indisputable. But to reverse the statement and infer, as our fathers did, that all suffering is due to sin just is not true. Yet everyone believed that once, for wrong ideas are amazingly tenacious. But everyone was wrong. The book of Job, that incomparable drama, wrestled with the problem as Job's "comforters" tried to defend their orthodox theological ideas against the obvious realities and experiences of life. Here, as in many other instances, life corrected theology in favor of the truth. Time invariably works on the side of truth.

Even in our own day we have seen this happen. How recently was isolationism popularly regarded as being the hallmark of Americanism. Today anyone who advocates this policy would be regarded as a noisy die-hard with not a leg to stand on.

Should this not give us ground for hope as we contemplate the many other false ideas, religious, political, racial, economic, which, like parasites, cling to the tree of life? Paul put it well. Said he: "If any man build upon this foundation gold, silver, precious stones, wood, hay, stubble; every man's work shall be made manifest: for the day shall declare it." (I Cor. 3:12-13.) The day, though often long in dawning, does declare the shoddy substitutes for what they are, while truth remains, sustained by its own inner integrity. There is an old proverb which says: "God made time but man made haste." In God's plan we must always set the verdict of the years against the hours. This certainly must have been the faith of the Master in his parable of the wheat and the tares: "Let both grow together until the harvest: and in the time of harvest I will say to the reapers, Gather ye together first the tares, and bind them in bundles to burn them: but gather the wheat into my barn." (Matt. 13:30.) Time is on the side of truth.

A second reason for believing in the triumphant nature of truth is that truth has a vitality and resilience greater than fact. Carlyle says: "There is an infinite significance in fact." He really should have said "in truth." It is worth noting that the Master did not say: "Ye shall know the facts, and the facts shall make you free." He said: "Ye shall know the truth" (John 8:32). "When Jesus declares that truth will . . . make us free, [he is] speaking, not of truth as agreement with external fact, but of truth as a condition of grace, a state of harmony. It is participation in reality, penetration in primary being." [34] When we forget

<hr>

[34] Sir S. Radhakrishnan, *Hibbert Journal*, July, 1946, p. 301.

this we do the cause of truth a great disservice. It is here that the literalist does such violence to scripture.

Take, for example, the story of the fall of man. Its factual details have rightly been questioned, but could anyone doubt the imperishable truths of that sublime story? Consider some of them: that God meant life to be beautiful; that the garden of every man's life grows its forbidden fruit; that life presents each man with inescapable moral choices; that temptation is real; that at the heart of all sin is deception; that we are morally responsible beings and so cannot escape the consequences of our deeds. Always to us comes the voice that spoke to Adam: "Where art thou?" (Gen. 3:9.) These are some of the truths in that story. It is too bad to lose them in our insistence upon its factual accuracy. Perhaps John Knox's words, used in a different connection, may be applicable here too when he says:

A cold, dispassionate study of the mightiest event in human history, whatever else it is, cannot be truly and fully historical. It may be accurate, but it is hopelessly inadequate. It may miss being false at any particular point, but it misses being true altogether.[35]

This story of creation, like so many in the Bible, does not miss being true, for it is true to life. It illumines so many deathless truths about man, and his life in this world, that the facts which were their medium of expression seem irrelevant. Facts are events in time; truth transcends time. Facts are the scaffolding, truth the building—shall we not say the "building of God, an house not made with hands, eternal" (II Cor. 5:1)?

[35] *Christ the Lord*, p. 5.

This assertion is vindicated by the simple observation that many of the verdicts which one age renders in favor of the facts, the more enlightened conscience of a succeeding age reverses in favor of the truth. Perchance the most significant example of this is the cross of Christ. If ever the facts were stacked against the truth, they were in that scene of the long ago. On the one side an all-powerful Roman state; a politically ambitious governor; a cunning, heartless but influential high priest; a court with its trumped-up charges; soldiers with their ready spears; an unthinking multitude, emotionally aroused and crying "Crucify him!"—all that on one side. And on the other? A Man hanging on a cross, defenseless and alone, his fearful friends cowering in the distance. The verdict was rendered in favor of the facts, which rode off in brazen triumph. But that Man on the cross represented Truth, imperishable Truth, and so time has reversed the verdict. The little actors, with their sinister and selfish purposes, who once strutted on the stage, have now gone off behind the wings somewhere, enjoying the sort of oblivion that history reserves for cruelty and injustice; and Truth, once on the scaffold, is now on the throne, because truth is more significant than fact. It is timeless and eternal.

The third reason for our belief that truth is imperishable and will triumph is that this faith has sustained the noblest souls in their finest hours.

> Not a truth has to art or to science been given,
> But brows have ached for it, and souls toil'd
> and striven.[36]

[36] Owen Meredith, *Lucile.*

And if this is true of art and science, how much more of the incomparable values of our faith. Here indeed some of the choicest and noblest souls have "toil'd and striven." There can be no doubt that the most creative souls in the world have been sustained by this deathless faith in the eternal consequence of truth. To defend it they have sacrificed popularity, possessions, position, yea, life itself. So John Hus, as one of his dearest friends, Palec, wavers and finally goes over to his enemies, says: "Palec is my friend, Truth is my friend: of the two it were only right to honor Truth most." [37] From then on not only Palec but other friends became his unsparing foes and he a martyr, gloriously symbolizing that triumphant faith which makes man but little lower than the angels. Similarly, Balthasar Hübmaier, as he faced his martyrdom, exclaimed: "Truth is immortal; and though for a long time she is imprisoned, scourged, crowned with thorns, crucified and buried, she will yet rise victorious on the third day and will reign and triumph." [38] Where would one begin or end in speaking of this noble army of martyrs, whose blood has been not only the seed of the church but a revelation of those eternal values in which alone man finds his true heritage and destiny?

Surely the witness of such dauntless and indomitable spirits, who loved truth more than life itself, cannot help but confirm our faith. One indeed has to decide whose verdict of life comes nearer to reality—that of the noblest souls in their best moments, or of those who grope and wallow. Whose verdict concerning life shall we accept, that of the cynic whose

[37] W. N. Schwarze, *John Hus,* p. 69.
[38] Walter Rauschenbusch, *Christianity and the Social Crisis,* p. 401.

sneer turns life sour, or of some radiant soul who, despite "the mystery of iniquity" (II Thess. 2:7), believes the best, lives it and so helps to create it? Who comes nearer reality, the skeptic in whose chilling atmosphere of disbelief and distrust the aspirations of men are blighted, or the man of faith who lives daringly, hopefully, victoriously, and faces death itself believing that beyond the darkness is the dawn? Who comes nearer reality, Pilate, who cynically asks "What is truth?" or Christ who goes to the cross, sustained by the unconquerable faith that truth is dearer than life, that truth *is* life in its fullest and richest expression? We shall stand with the saints, apostles, prophets, and martyrs, against the cynics, skeptics, the self-centered, or the self-indulgent.

It follows, as a sort of corollary, that to regard truth as indestructible and finally triumphant is to believe in God. "Homage to the ultimate values is the worship of God," says Dean Inge. It is instructive how many who lose faith in God find it again along the road of moral conviction. The nineteenth century, due to the progress of natural science and the birth of higher criticism, was an age of widespread doubt. Many religious thinkers groped their way through it. Robertson of Brighton was one of them. He came through his agony of doubt "by holding fast to those things which are certain still—the grand simple landmarks of morality." [39] So too Tennyson, when caught in the conflict of "our dearest faith; our ghastliest doubt," found faith restored in the moral consciousness.

[39] Stopford A. Brooke, *Life and Letters of Frederick W. Robertson*, I, p. 121.

Perplext in faith, but pure in deeds,
At last he beat his music out.

. . . .

Thus he came at length

To find a stronger faith his own.[40]

Robert Browning, whose poetry has done so much to sustain faith, made his appeal "from the intelligence to the moral consciousness." He rested in the conviction

that the universe "means intensely and means good," but, above all, that it means love, that "the All-Great" is "the All-Loving too." . . . It was a case of faith being driven back by intellectual difficulties upon its own last defences, and thus discovering what these defences actually are—the certainties of the moral consciousness.[41]

Bergson writes beautifully and truly when, in speaking of those whom he characterized as "the men of moral grandeur," he says:

It is in studying these great lives, in striving to experience sympathetically what they experience, that we may penetrate by an act of intuition to the life-principle itself. To pierce the mystery of the deep it is sometimes necessary to regard the heights. It is earth's hidden fire which appears at the summit of the volcano.[42]

Even so, it is the spiritual heights reached by the great souls of the race that reveal the deepest order of Reality

[40] *In Memoriam.*
[41] D. M. Baillie, *Our Faith in God,* pp. 155-57.
[42] *Mind-Energy* (Amer. ed.), p. 32.

which undergirds and sustains our values, that is to say, reveals God. For if there is one thing of which we may be certain it is that those who defend the truth are convinced it is not *their* truth which is being defended. They are merely responding to an obligation laid upon them by God. Their loyalty to truth is not just loyalty to some vague, abstract principle but loyalty to the God of Truth, whose cause they hold dearer than life. They sacrifice for truth because they believe that even though the odds are against them, God is on their side, and that God will not fail nor at long last be defeated. As the psalmist puts it:

> Truth springeth out of the earth;
> And righteousness hath looked down from heaven.
> Yea, Jehovah will give that which is good.
> (85:11-12 A.S.V.)

This was the faith of the early Christians. The odds were always against them. They were outnumbered; they faced a hostile government; they were objects of suspicion and persecution; they were stoned, imprisoned, thrown to the lions, slain; but they were unconquerable. They died saying, "If God be for us, who can be against us?" and "We are more than conquerors through him that loved us." (Rom. 8:31, 37.) They believed their cause unconquerable because they believed in the God of Truth, their refuge and strength, who is from everlasting to everlasting.

This too is our faith. The values for which we strive are not human inventions. They are neither optional nor arbitrary.

On the contrary they belong here and are organically related
to the very structure of the universe. In fighting for them

I am not fighting alone, against impossible odds, for a fantastically
hopeless cause, and with the paralysing suspicion in my heart
that it cannot really matter whether I win or lose. . . . Nay, rather
it is Reality's own battle that I am fighting, and the stars in their
courses are fighting with me and the very Force that moves them
is on my side. . . . And it is the only battle that matters in all the
world, and the prize is the only prize that will endure.[43]

As we think therefore of the brave men who have died for
truth we feel sure that they were not fighting for a lost cause.
The dawn for which they looked has not broken but it will
break. Light is stronger than darkness, for "God is light." God
is on the side of light. The good they envisioned has not come
but it will. Good will conquer evil, for "the Lord is good."
God is on the side of good. The truth they cherished is not
yet on the throne, but it will be. Truth is stronger than error.
God is "the God of truth." He is on the side of truth. Does this
mean that we may fold our hands and naïvely assume that
everything will come out all right? Not so. This faith of ours
presupposes that God will continue to find men who will love
truth, labor and sacrifice for it; yea, and if need be, die for
it. "These all died in faith, not having received the promises,
but having seen them afar off, . . . that they without us should
not be made perfect." (Heb. 11:13, 40.) "They without us"—
it cannot be accomplished *without us.*

We have noted that men find God in values which they

[43] John Baillie, *The Interpretation of Religion,* p. 326.

believe to be eternal, and that in devotion to these they express their loyalty to God. Time and again, however, we shall be reminding ourselves that "God, who at sundry times and in divers manners spake in time past unto the fathers by the prophets, hath in these last days spoken unto us by his Son" (Heb. 1:1). In all our discussion of truth the eye of faith will find in him its surest verification, its supreme fulfillment. "And we beheld his glory, the glory as of the only begotten of the Father, full of grace and truth." (John 1:14.) And those of us to whom that vision comes will have an answer to Pilate's question "What is truth?" For in the Man of Nazareth, his life and death, we shall see not only the embodiment of life's choicest values; we shall see God, who, through his righteous judgments and his tender mercies, seeks to bring his wayward children to a knowledge of the truth in which is our salvation.

II

TRUTH AS MORAL REALITY

WE are accustomed to regard truth as though it were primarily, if not solely, an affair of the intellect. Goodness, we say, has a moral quality, beauty an aesthetic quality, and truth a purely intellectual quality. This generalization, though plausible, is inaccurate. I shall endeavor to point out that morality is the basic ingredient of all truth, even of the truth which is regarded as the exclusive concern of the intellect. Moral reality is in fact life's primary and basic truth.

Kant said as much in his oft-quoted words: "Two things fill the mind with ever new and increasing admiration and awe, the oftener and the more steadily we reflect on them: the starry heaven above and the moral law within." [1] Elijah described the moral sense as "a still small voice" (I Kings 19:12), and the Master described it as "the light that is in thee" (Matt. 6:23). We frequently speak of it as "conscience." These are but different ways of describing this imponderable quality which is the image of God in man. I shall use the

---

[1] *Critique of Practical Reason*, ed. T. K. Abbott, 3rd ed., p. 260.

words "moral reality," "moral sense," and "conscience" interchangeably.

It is of course obvious that in the Judaic-Christian tradition truth is seldom, if ever, regarded as just an affair of the mind. When the psalmist prays: "O send out thy light and thy truth: let them lead me: let them bring me unto thy holy hill" (43:3), or when Zechariah says: "These are the things that ye shall do: Speak ye every man the truth to his neighbor; execute the judgment of truth and peace in your gates" (8:16), or when Malachi describes one by saying: "The law of truth was in his mouth, and iniquity was not found in his lips: he walked with me in peace and equity, and did turn many away from iniquity" (2:6), it is obvious that these writers stress both the ethical nature of truth and the realistic nature of the ethical as something more than that which is merely nominal, intellectual, or conceptual.

In the New Testament this is even more evident. "Brethren, if any of you do err from the truth, and one convert him, let him know, that he which converteth the sinner from the error of his way shall save a soul from death, and shall hide a multitude of sins." (Jas. 5:19-20.) The frequent use of the word truth attributed to the Master in the Fourth Gospel might very well indicate his interest in the intellectual life. An examination of his use of the word, however, makes it clear that he never thought of truth as though it were merely a matter of intellectual apprehension. Such statements as "Sanctify them in the truth: thy word is truth" (John 17:17 A.S.V.) or "Howbeit when he, the Spirit of truth, is come, he shall guide you into all the truth" (John 16:13 A.S.V.),

47

manifestly involve more than the intellect. They involve the whole man. Phillips Brooks is voicing the thought of the Master when he writes:

A "man of the truth" is something more than a man who knows the truth, whose intellect has seized it; that, we are sure, would be the very tamest paraphrase of the suggestive words. . . . A "man of the truth" is a man into all whose life the truth has been pressed till he is full of it, till he has been given to it, and it has been given to him.[2]

Jesus would agree that in the highest things the intellect can never work alone for the discovery of truth. "Not from simple brain to simple brain, as the reasoning of Euclid comes to its students, but from total character to total character, comes the New Testament from God to men."[3] Christianity maintains therefore that truth possesses a moral quality and so is revealed not to the mind alone but the whole personality.

But it is not only in Christianity that truth reveals its moral quality. Consider art. The real artist has some ethical framework within which his creative powers move, and so the liberty of the real artist never becomes license, and his imagination, though vivid, is never weird. We watch him at work, toning down this color or making that other one brighter, as though some unseen critic were looking over his shoulder, passing judgment on his effort, urging him on to do justice to his subject. It is the rampant individualism, which seemingly recognizes no objective aesthetic standard,

[2] *The Influence of Jesus,* p. 218.
[3] *Ibid.,* p. 234.

that justifies in part at least Dean Inge's saying that some modern art reminds him "of now the work of a very unpleasant child, now the first efforts of an African savage, and now the delirious hallucinations of an incurable lunatic." [4] The musician too conforms to some standard as he keeps playing a certain phrase over and over again until he feels he has caught the composer's intent. The poet tries "phrase and rhythm till at last the inexorable monitor is appeased." In artist, musician, or poet "there is something within . . . approving or condemning his execution till at last it says to him, 'That will do.'" There is, as a distinguished Victorian writer has said, "a scale of values in the soul." [5]

But this moral ingredient is present not only in the field of religion and aesthetics, where one might expect to find it, but even in that realm which we are wont to regard as the exclusive affair of the intellect—the field of science. Think now, not of science but of the scientist, without whom there could be no science. There are two facts which strongly indicate the bearing of morality on the field of scientific inquiry. The first is the presence in the scientist of what Huxley called "the fanaticism for veracity." By his use of pure reason the scientist may say, "This is true," or, "This is false," but the *impulse* that urges him, despite repeated failures, to stop at nothing short of the truth regardless of the cost in effort or sacrifice—is that purely intellectual? If it is, then the intellect is itself a moral phenomenon. "God forgive a scientist's passion," cried Pasteur. "Passion!" Surely that

---

[4] *Christian Ethics and Modern Problems,* p. 400.
[5] D. S. Cairns, *The Riddle of the World,* pp. 99-100.

BETHEL SEMINARY WEST
LIBRARY
6116 Arosa Street
San Diego, CA 92115-3902

cannot be confined within the category of "pure intellectualism," yet but for this passion for truth, "the fanaticism for veracity," which keeps the scientist on the straight and narrow way of disciplined effort, there would be no scientific discovery whatsoever.

The moral aspect of scientific truth is seen also in the hardships and hazards voluntarily undertaken by the scientist in achieving his goal. A scientific expedition to the polar regions is not undertaken and carried out by detached intellects but by men without whose heroism and almost reckless daring no scientific findings could be made. One thinks of Alfred Wegener, the German geophysicist who led an expedition to Greenland. When food was running low he quietly went out to die alone so that his aides might live a little longer—a deed of heroism which had been performed earlier by the brave Englishman Lawrence Oates, on Captain Scott's expedition to the South Pole in 1912.

The Brooklyn Bridge, one of the engineering triumphs of the early nineteenth century, is vastly more than a tribute to science, as though science were some abstract, coldly impersonal progeny of man's intellect. The Brooklyn Bridge is a monument to the dauntless courage and heroic sacrifice of two men, John Roebling, who first conceived the idea of the bridge, and Washington A. Roebling, his son, who built it. One of them gave his life, while the other contracted "the bends." He became partially paralyzed. His body was in constant pain, his voice gone. But what happened? He kept the work going. When he could no longer converse he wrote out his instructions, and with a rigid body "watched through field glasses the towers rise, the bridge take shape." Of what use would have been the scientific "know how" of these men without their stout hearts and indomitable wills?

Medical men also have exhibited this spirit. Take but one example. In the high Andes two diseases occurred, one a relatively mild one, and one a very serious one. Dr. Daniel A. Carrion believed they were two forms of the same disease. He inoculated himself with infectious material from a mild form, developed the severe form, and thereby proved their identity. He died of the infection. Such illustrations could be multiplied.

These and similar sacrificial exploits are not simply tributes to science, which is an abstraction, but to man, and not just to man's intellect but to his character—to the moral integrity that undergirds and inspires his intellectual efforts. Sometimes we speak of the intellect as though it were a contraption in the head which in turn rests as lightly and casually on the shoulders as a sparrow on a telephone wire. Even as the sparrow is wholly indifferent to, or oblivious of, the impulses that move along the wire, so is the head unaffected by what goes on in the rest of the human organism. Such a concept is false. One is almost tempted to say that pure intellectualism is pure nonsense. There just is not any such thing. The intellect is part of a man. It is affected by his ideals or lack of them, his emotions, his will, his motives—be they pure or corrupt. If a man should ever become a pure intellect he would not be a man but a freak. One would no longer trust his views on any subject, least of all on life. His outlook would be jaundiced.

If we wanted further proof that truth is not simply an affair of the intellect but that the deepest truth is moral and can be grasped only by the whole personality, it could be seen in the fact that just now when man has reached the pinnacle of his intellectual achievements, his position was never more precarious. Our amazing scientific advance has not made modern man happier, wiser, or more secure, but more apprehensive, jittery, and fearful. The atomic bomb, "Exhibit A" of man's intellectual prowess, now threatens to destroy him and all his works. "The only answer to atomic power is moral power." [6] Surely this should be proof enough that the key to man's knowledge of the truth does not lie in his mind alone, that though he "know all mysteries and all knowledge, . . . but have not love," it profiteth him nothing. (I Cor. 13:2.) As Hartley Burr Alexander writes:

God is man's resentment of the imperfections of his world—just as science is our resentment of the world's imbecilities. And God is our faith in moral sanity—just as science is our faith in intellectual sanity, *which itself to be sane must be included within the moral.* [7]

In moral reality, then, lies the keystone of the arch of life. No civilization has ever fallen because it lacked knowledge, but invariably because it lacked character. The great crises of life are induced not so much because men lack intelligence as because they lack integrity. If Sodom is to be saved ten *righteous* men must be found. The calamities that have be-

[6] D. Elton Trueblood, *Foundations for Reconstruction*, p. 8.
[7] *Truth and the Faith*, p. 311. Italics mine.

fallen mankind, from the days of Noah until now, spring inevitably from one major source—moral degeneration. When man's moral condition sinks below a certain level nothing on earth can halt his descent or avert his further deterioration or destruction save moral and spiritual regeneration. "And God saw that the wickedness of man was great in the earth, and that every imagination of the thoughts of his heart was only evil continually. . . . The earth also was corrupt before God, and the earth was filled with violence. And God looked upon the earth, and, behold, it was corrupt; for all flesh had corrupted his way upon the earth." (Gen. 6:5, 11-12.) Thus did the ancient writer of Genesis account for the coming of the flood. The people of Noah's time may, for all we know, have had high I.Q.'s, but it takes more than that to stave off calamity.

The problem of man today, therefore, as it has ever been, is not the problem of truth as an intellectual phenomenon. Man's security, indeed his survival, depends primarily upon his ability to come to grips with truth as basic moral reality. This reality is organically related to his life upon the earth, and cannot possibly be evaded. We are concerned to increase knowledge, and rightly so, since there is nothing divine about ignorance. But we have vastly more to fear from the morally stupid and the spiritually illiterate than from the uneducated since, as we now clearly see, education without integrity is a dubious blessing. The Bible is most realistic here. It does not say that the primary problem of man lies in his mind and that knowledge will solve it. It insists that man's primary problem rests in his sinful heart and stubborn will, and that his salvation lies in God's redeeming grace.

Let me now, in the second place, point out two of the characteristic marks of this inner moral sense. One is its universality. No man is ever wholly without it. "In fact," writes Lewis Richard Farnell, "we may find primitive tribes without any clear belief in personal deities; but we find none without morality." [8] This is not to say that in all men everywhere the moral sense is equally developed. It is, however, present in every one. Even gangsters have some moral code, since "there is honor among thieves." Might we not say that the possession of the moral sense is partly at least what is meant by being created in the image of God? That image is stamped on all men everywhere.

Of course the moral sense, though the mark of God, is not an unerring guide. Cruel wrongs have been committed by conscientious people. The Pharisees in their bitter antagonism to Jesus were unquestionably conscientious. The Inquisition was instituted by conscientious folk.

Kipling says somewhere that there is only one thing more terrible in action than a company of desperadoes officered by a half-dozen young daredevils, and that is a regiment of Scotch Presbyterians who rise from their knees and go into battle convinced that they are about to do the will of God.[9]

So too Lecky, in his *History of European Morals*, writes: "Philip II and Isabella . . . inflicted more suffering in obedi-

[8] *Attributes of God*, p. 207.
[9] Willard L. Sperry, *What We Mean by Religion*, p. 72.

ence to their consciences than Nero and Domitian in obedience to their lusts." [10]

Not only so, but, as often happens, this universal phenomenon conscience too often acts as a *post eventum*—it makes one see the wrong more clearly after the wrong has been committed than before or even during its commission. Sin, like some deadening drug, tends to stupefy and make quiescent the moral judgment. The prodigal goes lightheartedly into the far country; it is not till he has reached journey's end that remorse, regret, and shame begin their work. John Kelman refers to this as "one of the deepest mysteries of Providence."

Looking back upon the tragedy of sin men feel that they have been cheated, . . . that their conscience has neither principles nor good sense nor even manners. They feel that if it had spoken before, as it so savagely speaks afterwards, they had been saved from life's tragedies. [11]

This is unfortunate. But there is no more justification for condemning wholesale our moral judgment because of its imperfection than for condemning our minds because sometimes when we think we are reasoning we are only rationalizing. This simply means that our consciences need educating even as do our minds.

We admit therefore that the moral sense, though the mark of God, is not an infallible guide even in the best of us. In primitive peoples it is naturally less educated; hence practices or behavior patterns which they accept as right and proper,

[10] I, 251.
[11] *The Foundations of Faith*, p. 132.

were we unethical enough to adopt, would land us in jail. The point, however, is this: no matter how men may differ about what is right or what is wrong, the faculty which distinguishes between the quality of rightness and the quality of wrongness is universally present in all men. The lowest society has some moral standards because all men have the moral sense. The moral sense is universal.

Another characteristic of the conscience is that it speaks with authority. It possesses an imperious quality. It not only says, "This is the way," but adds, "Walk ye in it." This inner voice may be "still" and "small" but it speaks commandingly. It puts one under obligation. It may be true that the modern man no longer believes that there is an immortal essence presiding like a king over his appetites. But there is, whether he believes it or not.

It makes a difference to everything that he [man] thinks or does, whether he has to live out his life in a world which has no meaning or value beyond what he himself gives to it, or whether there is in the universe outside himself a perfection to which he may aspire, a voice to which he may answer, a love to which he may respond, a grace by which he may be sustained.[12]

The proof that we live in such a world is seen in at least two ways. When, for example, we live self-contained and self-sufficient lives and so fail through prayer and meditation to open our lives to the spiritual resources that God has made available, how impoverished our lives become. Or again, when we act as though we were a law unto ourselves, as

[12] *Christian News Letter,* No. 291, p. 5.

though there were no will in this universe greater than our own to whom we owe obedience, into what painful paths of frustration and futility, if not stark tragedy, are we led! For conscience, God's voice to the soul, does not, when it is flouted, abdicate and, as some dethroned monarch, go into exile; rather it maintains its imperious character as it saddles us with remorse, disillusionment, and regret. And should we persist in our evil ways until conscience is no longer heard at all, then the price is most fearful. For if we become impervious to the divine intimations shall we not well-nigh have defaced God's image within us, and so have lost that which makes us men rather than brutes? O. Hobart Mowrer, Harvard psychologist, in speaking to a group of his colleagues recently, said that instead of calling the conscience the villain which bottles up the guilt-stricken patient and his impulses, we ought to help the patient "to turn a good ear to conscience" and "to do business with it." [13]

Many responsible psychologists are coming increasingly to this position. They are now saying that in many, if not most, instances mental or nervous disorders are neither biological nor psychological in their origin, but moral and spiritual. They spring from some moral problem of good or evil, right or wrong, which we have compromised or have in one way or another been unable successfully to resolve. We may play fast and loose with this inner voice, but we can never escape the consequences of so doing. The consequences are invariably severe.

[13] *Cleveland Plain Dealer,* February 22, 1947.

We have noted that moral reality is the deepest truth. We have observed two of its characteristic marks: its universality and imperiousness. Now, in the third place, let us ask: "Whence came this moral sense? What is its source?"

The first possible source is nature; the moral sense is of the earth earthly. Perhaps the best-known exponent of this point of view is Rousseau, the father of romantic morality. No doubt Rousseau has made a contribution to human progress and does not deserve all the condemnation that has been placed on him by moralists, yet Dean Inge may be partly right in saying: "The influence of this sentimental theoretician has perhaps been more pernicious than that of any other man who has ever lived." [14] Rousseau taught that man, body and soul, was the product of nature and was by nature good. He was not concerned about original sin; rather he rejoiced in original nature, which he regarded as wholly good. As far as Rousseau and his followers were concerned, morality as we know it was completely nonexistent. Its disappearance was accomplished by a very simple device, namely, that of identifying conscience with the instincts. Conscience then lost its imperiousness. The sense of moral obligation was done away. "Ought" lost its meaning. Natural impulses became the basis of all morality and all discipline. This meant that there was no morality and no discipline. To be good one needed only to be natural. If I may be permitted to say so, Rousseau's philosophy in a nutshell is "Ain't nature grand!" and the peak of human achievement reached in "doing what comes

[14] *Christian Ethics and Modern Problems*, p. 249.

naturally." It is society which, by its artificial and unnatural restraints, has corrupted man and perverted what, if nature had her unimpeded way, would be a "beautiful soul." Renan was only re-echoing Rousseau's philosophy when he wrote:

Morality has been conceived up to the present in a very narrow spirit, as obedience to a law, as an inner struggle between opposite laws. As for me, I declare that when I do good I obey no one, I fight no battle and win no victory. The cultivated man has only to follow the delicious incline of his inner impulses.[15]

The fallacy of this philosophy became evident almost immediately in the ghastly harvest of disillusionment, despair, and disgust reaped by Rousseau's ardent followers. His philosophy, based on the innate goodness of man and the loveliness of nature, probably produced the greatest literature of disillusionment and despair the world has ever seen. To follow the movement from Rousseau to the present day is to realize that the fruit of undisciplined living is not joy but sorrow, not gaiety but gloom.

Nor should we forget the present day. Not in the lifetime of some of us did our American life and culture strike a lower level than in the years following World War I—the 1920's and after. Under the widespread influence of that monstrous half-truth behavioristic psychology, which all but destroyed our moral responsibility, we lost our souls if not our minds. The gospel of self-expression came into hideous flower. Restraint was thrown to the winds. Every Tom, Dick, and Harry

[15] Quoted by Irving Babbitt, *Rousseau and Romanticism*, p. 133, from *Avenir de la Science*, p. 354.

59

felt that his first duty under God was to express himself—and such selves as we expressed! Our literature became obsessed with muckraking and debunking, all in the name of "realism" so-called, which we identified with vulgarism and filth. It was Rousseau again in another garb. Once more we were told: "Be yourself; be natural." But while the self is a part of nature, it can never be wholly explained on the basis of nature. Man is a child of nature yet in some mysterious way transcends nature. He has a moral sense which nature has not given. Because of this, whenever he tries to live as though he were no different from the brutes, he never succeeds in becoming like them but invariably sinks below them. The very image of God which makes him a little lower than the angels, when betrayed, makes him lower than the brutes. It is evident therefore that we are compelled to rule out nature as the source of the moral sense. For when we act as though we were nothing more than children of Mother Nature we become something far less.

Another possible source of the moral sense is society. The still small voice, so it is said, is not the voice of nature but of man, corporate man. Conscience is the result of the customs and laws which society has imposed on the individual through centuries of group pressure. The moral sense is just as man-made as an automobile or a refrigerator. Now, that society plays a part in the development of conscience is admitted. The word "morals" comes from *mos*, plural *mores*, which means customs. It is one thing, however, to say society gives us our moral *standards*, and a wholly different matter to say it gives us our moral *sense*. A college may provide an

60

education, but it does not give us our minds. A scientist works with the laws of nature but he never created one of them. They are given. So man works with the moral laws of the universe or against them—but he does not create them, they were given. To say that conscience is merely an "inherited prejudice" or "transmitted racial experience" is, as William Ernest Hocking has pointed out, defective thinking, since, as he wisely observes, "Mental traits that come down to us from antiquity grow weaker as we recede from the source," while conscience, on the contrary, grows more sensitive, more enlightened, "moves ahead of ancestral requirements, and hence cannot be explained away as a mere biological inheritance." [16]

Furthermore, the voice of conscience, as I have said, is an imperious voice. It speaks with authority; it commands. One wonders if man, voluntarily and knowingly, would have imposed such a restriction upon himself. Indeed, *could* he even if he would? Is not Karl Heim right when he says that man cannot lay an unconditional on his own will, by his own will? Fortunately we do not need to depend on abstract arguments alone in attempting to answer that question. There are two facts which, from a practical common-sense point of view, indicate that society cannot be regarded as the ultimate source of the moral sense.

One is that if the moral sense derives from society, it is difficult to explain how the individual so often sits in judgment on the very society from which presumably he derived his moral judgment.

[16] *Types of Philosophy*, p. 147 ff.

Civilization is so far from being identical with morality that every advance in civilization is merely a further demand upon our personal discernment to differ from its errors and oppose its corruptions.[17]

The prophets are singularly instructive here. They were not echoes of their nation's voice but the voice of God speaking to the nation: "Thus saith the Lord" was their unfailing sanction. To the prophets moral insights were regarded as most valid revelations of God. They did not try to "give the people what they want," mouthing watery and weak platitudes; their loyalty was never just to the people but to the eternal Reality behind and above the human scene. In the light of that Reality they judged themselves and brought society to judgment. "I saw the Lord . . . , high and lifted up. . . . Then said I, . . . I am a man of unclean lips, and I dwell in the midst of a people of unclean lips." (Isa. 6:1, 5.) To try to explain the moral insights of the prophets as an expression of the nation's mind is palpably absurd, since it was the immoral conduct of the nation that they constantly resisted and attacked. So Jeremiah says: "I am become a laughing-stock all the day, every one mocketh me. For as often as I speak, I cry out; I cry, Violence and destruction! because the word of Jehovah is made a reproach unto me, and a derision, all the day. And if I say, I will not make mention of him, nor speak anymore in his name, then there is in my heart as it were a burning fire shut up in my bones, and I am weary with forbearing, and I cannot contain."

[17] John Oman, *Grace and Personality*, p. 66.

(Jer. 20:7-9 A.S.V.) What is true of the prophets is also true of the martyrs. One of the best known of them, Paul, was quite explicit on this matter. Said he: "I make known to you, brethren, as touching the gospel which was preached by me, that it is not after man. For neither did I receive it from man, nor was I taught it, but it came to me through revelation of Jesus Christ." (Gal. 1:11-12 A.S.V.)

The Master, however, stands as the supreme example of the inadequacy of ascribing moral and spiritual insights to society. "O Jerusalem, Jerusalem, that killest the prophets, . . . how often would I, . . . and ye would not!" (Matt. 23:37.) And "killest the prophets," mark you, not because their moral judgments were not as good as Jerusalem's but because they were so much better. How could we explain the act of Jesus going to his cross, constrained by the great compulsion "the Son of man must" (Mark 8:31), as an expression of the community mind, when the impulse that sent him there, and the values for which he died, were precisely those of which the community in general knew little or nothing? The collectivist theory of morals breaks down for the same reason as does Durkheim's collectivist theory of religion.

The whole tendency of religion and morality to reject the verdicts of society as not ultimately authoritative in their sphere shows how inadequate it is to attempt to trace religious feeling (or the moral sense, I may add) to nothing deeper than the impession made on the individual by the group.[18]

We are probably much nearer the truth when we say that

[18] A. Campbell Garnett, *A Realistic Philosophy of Religion*, p. 68.

63

it was conscience that made society possible than to say that conscience is the product of social forces. "That which, back of it all, invests right with rightness and wrong with wrongness is something intrinsic to the soul." [19]

There is, however, another common-sense reason for believing that the moral sense is intrinsic in the soul, namely, that the collectivist theory of morality leads man inevitably to demonic behavior. The Victorian philosopher T. H. Green declared: "No individual can make a conscience for himself. He always needs a society to make it for him." [20] But the difficulty with such a statement is that when you make society the creator of morality you inevitably make society morally irresponsible and so open the door for tyranny, since society then becomes the ultimate. In such an event society brings the individual to judgment, but nothing or no one brings society to the bar of judgment. It judges but itself is never judged.

Herein lies the tragedy and terror of totalitarianism. The group sits in judgment on the individual but itself is responsible to nothing or no one save its own arrogant and brutal self-will. It then becomes a law unto itself. When, however, the group fails to realize that it stands under the judgment of an ultimate truth that transcends it and holds it accountable, it becomes demonic. Is not this the curse of our time? The Nazis made race the ultimate, the Fascists the state, the Communists the proletarian class. These totalitarian schemes recognize no authority beyond their own

[19] Roy A. Burkhart, *The Church and the Returning Soldier*, p. 160.
[20] *Prolegomena to Ethics*, p. 387.

arrogant, perverted will. This of course means that inevitably they betray and crucify the truth. For it is now writ large in letters of fire and blood across the face of this stricken earth that whenever the group, whatever its name, owns responsibility to no power beyond itself, tyranny, with all its hideous brood, is turned loose upon the earth. We cannot believe then that the moral sense derives from society, for when society acts as if it were a moral ultimate, and so plays God, it invariably behaves like the devil.

It appears that when we rest the moral sense on the bosom of Mother Nature, as did Rousseau, we become worse than brutes, and when we posit it on the collective social will, we become devils; but in neither case do we remain men. We maintain therefore that neither nature nor society gives the right answer and we are led to conclude that the voice within is not the echo of nature's voice, nor the conceited expression of human arrogance, but is rather the voice of the living God.

> Man's justice from the all-just Gods was given,
> A light that from some upper fount did beam,
> Some better archetype whose seat was Heaven.[21]

"In the act of conscience," writes James Martineau, "we are immediately introduced to the Higher than ourselves that gives us what we feel." [22] Or, as the book of Proverbs puts it, in Dr. Moffatt's translation, "Man's conscience is the lamp

[21] Author unknown. Quoted by Lewis Richard Farnell, *Attributes of God*, p. 205.
[22] *A Study of Religion*, II, 27.

of the Eternal, flashing into his inmost soul." (Prov. 20:27.) So if, as we have argued, God is our guarantee that truth is imperishable, we may say now that truth is our assurance that God is real, ever-present and inescapable. This moral universe rests on the being of God, who is its Creator and Sustainer. To say this is of course to say that morality has cosmic significance. It inheres in the organic nature of the universe.

Some of course do not share this faith. They regard man as a child of nature, and nature as unmoral. Man is therefore, spiritually speaking, an orphan. Nature supplies his physical needs with lavish hand but her cupboard is as bare of spiritual values as was Mother Hubbard's of bones. Although man is therefore urged to fight for his values, he knows he fights a losing battle. He has no ally save his own reluctant will. He is like a man trying to grow a crop in a soil to which it is not indigenous and in a climate wholly uncongenial. His attempt therefore is arbitrary and artificial, and in the long last will prove futile. This is the verdict of the materialist himself.

It would seem to me that human life and experience do not support this verdict. For example, the warmhearted humanist Vincent Sheean, in referring to the period following World War I, writes:

Whatever morality may be—and it seems probable that it was never anything but a series of convenient arrangements—its recognizable influence had vanished from the more conspicuous aspects of life in Paris and London in the 1920's.[23]

[23] *Personal History,* p. 310.

66

Incidentally, I do not see why Sheean should have omitted Washington, unless he wanted to infer that, in the period of which he writes, morality had vanished from there sooner! But is not this an oversimplification of the significance of moral reality? For if morality were only "a series of convenient arrangements," then when it "vanishes" no serious results should obtain. We all know what it means to be inconvenienced: the car does not start or the train is late or the fuse blows out. Such experiences are annoying or irksome. But they are not serious. When, however, we flout or betray the moral law the results are of a quite different sort. We seem to set in motion forces that we cannot stop. We set up a sort of spiritual chain reaction. The situation deteriorates until it explodes in darkest tragedy.

Two world wars in one generation are evidence enough. This is no "inconvenience" that we are experiencing. This is the judgment of God upon a generation that is so morally stupid that having eyes it sees not. For the plain fact is that whenever London, Paris, Washington, or Moscow, individually or collectively, substitutes trickery, expedience, or treachery for what Robertson of Brighton called "the grand simple landmarks of morality," the result is that, like some blind Samson, we shake loose the foundations of the temple of our civilization and send it crashing down in wholesale devastation and death upon ourselves. That is why the morally mature are never so sure of God as in those very periods when the superficial are least sure of him. For the mature see chaos and tragedy against the background of the moral integrity of a universe upheld by the very being

67

of God. To resist or betray the moral realities of such a universe is, as now we clearly see, to court disaster. As John Bright once put it:

The moral law was not written for men alone in their individual character, but it was written as well for nations. . . . If nations reject and deride that moral law, there is a penalty which will inevitably follow. It may not come at once, it may not come in our lifetime; but, rely upon it, the great Italian is not a poet only, but a prophet, when he says:
"The sword of heaven is not in haste to smite,
Nor yet doth linger." [24]

When we treat morality as though it were a political football to be kicked around, we are the ones who get kicked around. When we live as though we made the moral laws and so can break, amend, or repeal them at will, we do not live—we die. The plain truth is that "we can play the moral game, but we do not make the moral rules." [25] Writes A. E. Taylor:

Serious living is no more compatible with the belief that the universe is indifferent to morality than serious and arduous pursuit of truth with the belief that truth is a human convention or superstition.[26]

Moral reality therefore not only reveals the deepest truth about man but also about the universe which is his home.

[24] Quoted by George Otto Trevelyan, *Life of John Bright*, p. 275.
[25] *Crozer Quarterly*, July, 1930, p. 286.
[26] *Faith of a Moralist*, I, 61.

It leads us, as I have said, to the God who is its Creator and Sustainer. Through the sense of moral obligation man is made aware that his role in this universe is not that of a landlord but a tenant. The last word is with God.

Now finally let us consider the bearing of what has been said upon the gospel we preach. Ours is indeed a glorious gospel. "We preach Christ crucified, . . . Christ the power of God, and the wisdom of God." (I Cor. 1:23-24.) We preach "the unsearchable riches of Christ" (Eph. 3:8), the gospel of God's unmerited love and redeeming grace, the length and breadth, the depth and height of which passes our knowledge. From this gospel of redeeming grace, symbolized by the cross, has come our theology with its doctrines, dogmas, and ecclesiastical policies and practices. The question I now raise is: "What is the relationship between truth as moral reality and the truth of our theology?" Let us consider Sinai as the symbol of moral reality, and Calvary as that of our theology. What then is the relationship between Sinai, the mount of the moral law, and Calvary, the mount of redeeming grace?

Of one thing we may be sure: there cannot be any antagonism or conflict between them. Both are revelations of the eternal God. The same God who "made known his ways unto Moses" (Ps. 103:7) has "spoken unto us in his Son" (Heb. 1:2). Sinai and Calvary therefore cannot be in antagonism to one another, for God never contradicts himself. We are rightly impatient with the type of liberalism that would reduce the gospel to the sort of moralism one would expect from Marcus Aurelius or Epictetus. On the other

69

hand we might well be unimpressed with the type of theology that keeps its head so high in the clouds as to belittle, if not scorn, morality. The gospel is not morality. But this is because it is more than morality. We must not act as though it were less.

As Christians we have often done just that. Warned the Master: "Except your righteousness shall exceed the righteousness of the scribes and Pharisees, ye shall in no case enter into the kingdom of heaven." (Matt. 5:20.) Calvary does exceed Sinai just as far as love exceeds law. The righteousness of the scribes and Pharisees was legal. It consisted too often in the meticulous performance of certain rites and ceremonies that were largely, if not wholly, unrelated to moral and ethical reality. The righteousness Jesus preached and lived was, on the contrary, rooted in moral reality. He had little or no patience, as well we know, with those who emphasized the trivia of religion to the neglect of the weightier matters. He was in line with the prophetic tradition which stemmed from Amos and Hosea, and has continued even until now. The prophets sought to rescue religion on the one hand from the corrupting influences resulting from its compromises and alliances with secularism and privilege, and on the other from the empty formalism and ecclesiastical dry rot which inevitably overtakes religion when it dodges the moral realities. Jesus faced those realities. Has not his church down the ages often failed to do so?

I shall now mention three results that would obtain if our theology were kept in closer touch with morality.

For one thing, as our theology becomes more informed

with moral reality, would not God be more real to us? The
first question of God to man—Adam—was: "Where art thou?"
(Gen. 3:9.) Is it a coincidence that this question was pro-
voked by man's involvement in a moral crisis? Is not the
moral sense the growing edge of our awareness of God? So
it seems the Master thought. Consider his conversation with
the rich young ruler. "Good Master," said the ruler, "What . . .
shall I do, that I may have eternal life?" (Matt. 19:16.) One
feels certain that the answer he received was not the one
he had expected, and must have surprised him greatly. For
from these lofty thoughts of eternal life Jesus brought him
back to the moral law: "If thou wilt enter into life, keep the
commandments." (Matt. 19:17.) As though to say: "That is
the starting point, you have to begin there." As Professor E.
F. Scott puts it: "His teaching, as we have now come to see,
was not mystical but practical. He knew of nothing that
could be placed higher than the moral demands." [27]

Another incident is equally illuminating. Passing once
through Samaria he engaged a Samaritan woman in conversation. It was indeed an amazing conversation, marked
by some of his profoundest spiritual insights. He spoke to
her of the "living water" which when one truly partakes of
it "shall be in him a well of water springing up into everlasting life" (John 4:14.) The woman was so impressed that
she said: "Sir, give me this water, that I thirst not, neither
come hither to draw. Jesus saith unto her, Go, call thy
husband" (John 4:15-16). And I suppose she must have

[27] *The Ethical Teachings of Jesus*, p. 38.

thought, whether she said so or not: "Why bring that up?"
She had had five of them. "And he whom thou now hast is
not thy husband." (John 4:18.)

Here again, you see, in discussing the "living water," one
of his most mystical and deeply spiritual insights, Jesus
brought the would-be disciple back to earth. The "water
springing up into everlasting life" would mean little or
nothing to one the inner waters of whose life were morally
polluted. Jesus' teaching was barbed. It always stuck into
what was most real in the individual, his moral sense. This
man who has given us the loftiest, the most transcendent
concepts of truth, so high that we cannot attain unto them,
kept his feet solidly on the ground. Theology may soar like
an airplane to great heights, but the plane, remember, takes
off from the solid earth and always against the wind. Moral
reality was the bedrock truth upon which Jesus based his
message. "True spiritual religion is a development, not of
magical religion, but of the moral life." [28] Christianity is more
than morality. It is not less.

This emphasis of the Master on moral reality should be
particularly helpful in the religious education of young
people. The religious casualties among young people, college young people in particular, are well known to us. That
they should experience "growing pains," pass through a period
of spiritual orientation due to the enlarging of their intellectual horizons, is to be expected. Nor need it be regretted.
But why so many who lose their religion altogether? Part

[28] George Tyrrell, *Christianity at the Cross-Roads,* p. 128.

of this is no doubt the professor's fault. It is the business of the educator to make the student think, to disturb, even to the point of upsetting him with the challenge of a larger truth. But I am thinking now of the "educator" whose approach is almost wholly negative. He tears down but never builds up. He takes a fiendish delight in destroying every vestige of faith among the immature. This is not only unsportsmanlike but is, in my judgment, the poorest sort of pedagogy.

Teachers, however, are not alone to blame. We often lose our religion, strangely enough, because we never had it, and we never had it because it was never related to what is most real in us—the moral sense. I sometimes think that the first step in teaching the Christian religion should be a strong introductory course in morality. There is a difference, as John Baillie points out, between "moral religion (which is the best religion) and moralistic religion (which represents a declension)." [29] One can be moral without being Christian, but one cannot be Christian without being moral. We mightily respect the laws of God in nature. We know we disobey them at our peril. But do we really believe that there are moral laws which work as inexorably? Whether we do or not, the fact is that Amos' plumb line is a symbol of a universe that is "morally on the square," and so will not and cannot sustain our crooked ways. This is as indisputable and inescapable a fact as Newton's principle of gravitation. We cannot ignore the one any more than the other and live.

[29] *The Interpretation of Religion,* p. 304.

This may seem as elementary as the three R's; yes, and it is as basic. Without it what comes after does not make sense, is not real. To be sure, God has given a fuller revelation of himself than in the moral law. He has spoken in Christ. But that is an advanced course. One wonders if the God of the Incarnation will mean much to a person who has not first found the God who speaks in the still small voice within. Can the God of theology ever be real to one who has not first confronted the God of morality? The man who defined God as an "oblong blur" had never related him to the moral realities of his experience.

"Surely the Lord is in this place; and I knew it not." (Gen. 28:16.) The surprise of Jacob sprang from the fact that he found God where, theologically speaking, he was not supposed to be. For Jacob was outside the boundaries of his country, and, according to the inadequate ideas of his time, when you left your country you left your God behind. But God is always greater than our theologies. Even the heaven of heavens cannot contain him. "Surely the Lord is in this place"—"this place" far removed from temple, Bible, altar, officiating priests, and all the symbols and practices which were labeled "religious." But if we cannot find God in "this place," the place where we study and toil, where we earn our daily bread, the place where we struggle with temptation or try to resolve honorably some moral problem in which we are involved; if we cannot find God in these experiences which are most real to us and unavoidable, shall we find him at all? "If I have told you earthly things, and ye believe not,

74

how shall ye believe, if I tell you of heavenly things?" (John 3:12.)

The Sermon on the Mount is incomparable. Its spiritual insights are unmatched. But that too is a postgraduate course. It will mean little to one who does not know the Ten Commandments. The man who does not know the meaning of "Thou shalt not covet" (Exod. 20:17), is not likely to get much from "Blessed are the poor in spirit: for theirs is the kingdom of heaven" (Matt. 5:3), or "Whosoever shall compel thee to go a mile, go with him twain" (Matt. 5:41). But we cannot go the second mile unless, or until, we have gone the first. First the blade, then the ear, then the full corn. Such is the law of growth, physical and spiritual. We cannot jump or skip the steps in the spiritual world any more than in the natural. The fuller revelation presupposes what precedes. It is not without significance that Phillips Brooks concludes a chapter on theology by saying:

Every change in religious thought ought to justify itself by a deepened and extended morality. . . . The manifestations of devoutness are variable and mistakable. The manifestations of moral life are in comparison with them invariable and clear. . . . For every new form of religious thinking it is a blessed thing that, full of its first fresh enthusiasm, it is compelled to pass along the road where the old, old solemn judges sit who have judged all the ages, the judges before whose searching gaze many an ardent young opinion has withered away and known its own worthlessness, the judges who ask of every comer the same unchanging question, "Can you make men better men?" No conceit of spirituality or wisdom must make any new opinion think it can escape that test. He who leaves the plain road where the great judges sit, and thinks that he can get around behind them and come into the road again beyond where they are sitting is sure to fall into some slough of subtlety and be seen of men no more.[30]

But keeping theology in closer touch with morality would not only make religion more real to the individual but also more socially effective. "Though they keep up a form of religion, they will have nothing to do with it as a force." (II Tim. 3:5 Moffatt.) Christianity, as we know it, is so often like an old castle, outwardly imposing but ineffective. Once the castle struck terror into the heart of an attacking foe, but no more. Guns are there but harmless. Tourists peer into their rusty barrels. The form is there, the force has gone. Is that not too largely true of Christianity? "What difference does Christianity make?" we are often asked. "Why, despite all these hundreds of years of Christian preaching and teaching do we still have wars and race conflicts, economic injustice, and all the evils that plague us?" Is the answer that we have never taken seriously enough the ethical teachings of Jesus; that our theology has not been in close enough touch with moral reality?

I recall a story my mother used to tell us of a pious grocer who lived above his place of business. He would on occasion call down to his clerk and say: "James."

"Yes, sir."

"Have you watered the milk?"

"Yes, sir."

"Have you pumpkined the butter?"

[30] *Essays and Addresses*, p. 230.

"Yes, sir."

"And put chicory in the coffee?"

"Yes, sir."

"Then come up to worship!"

Too much of that sort of thing goes on in our Christian civilization. "Business is business." "You must not mix religion and politics." This means that religion is shunted off on a siding while the traffic flows on the main line without its direction or control.

It was not always thus. D. R. Sharpe, Rauschenbusch lecturer for 1948, wrote in a letter to me:

In ancient and medieval cities the church and state were linked in a powerful combination. Together they prescribed the economic life and exercised rigid control over it. In the modern city the church has lost control over the economic order and has been pushed to the periphery of urban life. This was due to a combination of forces. A partial list of these forces would include: the complexity of capitalistic industry, the liberation of intellectual life, furthered by such factors as Darwin's *Origin of Species* and his evolutionary hypothesis, the separation of church and state and the consequent loss of power over economic life, and the general drift in the direction of freedom from restraints. The laissez-faire economic and political philosophy further weakened the position of the church.

Then too the frontier movement had come to an end. The church had marched across the country and planted itself wherever new country was opened up: In this Protestantism displayed courage, foresight, and Christian statesmanship. It kept theology and ethics closely linked.

Now with the geographical frontiers closed, with the complexity and confusion of urban life, with the masses of people cut adrift from their old moorings, theology has become divorced from life, and Protestantism left helpless in the face of tragic need on the one hand and its greatest opportunity for practical service to humanity on the other hand.

That service can be rendered only as our religion becomes more ethical and our ethics more religious. This may be partly what J. S. Whale contemplates when he writes: "Any present-day theology which has not a revolutionary sociology as part of its implicit logic is not truly Christian." [31]

Here again how instructive is the example of Jesus! The phrase "the ethical teachings of Jesus" has become a by-word. This is not to say that Jesus was only a teacher of ethics— far from that. Sever his ethical insights from his profound faith in God and they would be the hallucinations of a distraught mind. With the Master, however, theology and ethics were one and inseparable. "The Word was made flesh." (John 1:14.) "The life was the light of men." (John 1:4.) It is impossible to tell where Jesus' theology stops and his ethics begin. They are the warp and woof of his very being.

This is evident from his teaching. Even if we bring our gift to the altar and there remember that our brother has aught against us, we must leave the gift at the altar, go first and be reconciled to the brother, then come and offer our gift. If, however, men allowed their religious observances to obscure or detract from their moral obligations, Jesus invariably stood with the moral as against the religious. "It was his insistence on the moral as against the religious obligations

[31] James S. Stewart, *Heralds of God*, p. 97.

78

which excited the hostility of the scribes and priests and led them to compass his death." [32] If his teaching like a barb stuck into what was most real in the individual, his moral sense, it also reached into what was most meaningful between the individual and his brother, his ethical relationships. A clever lawyer tried once to involve him in abstract discussions about neighborliness. He fared no better than did the woman at the well. Jesus answered his question not with a finespun definition of neighborliness in the abstract, but with a simple story illuminating a deed in which neighborliness is interpreted in terms of the moral obligations that bind men to one another.

The Master took this stand in the interest of religion, since to his way of thinking any religion that evades or betrays moral reality is not religion at all. So unmistakable was his emphasis in such instances that sometimes men in his presence would instinctively recall their wrong relationships and offer to right them, like Zacchaeus, who volunteered: "Lord, the half of my goods I give to the poor; and if I have wrongfully exacted aught of any man, I restore fourfold" (Luke 19:8 A.S.V.)

Does the presence of the Christian church in society today make men recall the importance of their ethical dealings? Is it not true that the Christian church, by and large, has often allowed its preoccupation with theological and ecclesiastical matters to obscure or sidetrack the moral and ethical implications which are the very crux of the human problem? How

[32] Ernest Findlay Scott, *Ethical Teachings of Jesus*, p. 37.

79

often in history has the church contended with issues so barren, on battlegrounds so remote, as to have had little relevance to life. The church down the ages has been guilty of the same evil for which the Master condemned the church of his day—tithing "mint and anise and cummin" and omitting "the weightier matters of the law" (Matt. 23:23).

In saying this I am not of course trying to minimize the importance of theology. Every religion must have a theology. A religion without a theology would be like a fish without bones—a jellyfish. By the same token, however, theology without the moral and ethical implications of prophetic religion is bones without the fish. Too often have our theological conflicts been just that barren and unproductive. In the perspective of history it would, for the most part, have been much better if the church, in the words of Edmund Gosse, had "let sleeping dogmas lie." If through the ages the church could have become as hot and bothered over the pressing moral and ethical issues of life as she has been over theological and ecclesiastical matters, the "promise of his coming" (II Pet. 3:4) would be much nearer to fulfillment. Raymond Calkins writes:

What often brings Christianity into disrepute in the modern mind is the spectacle of men and women talking about grace and faith and the rare experiences of the Spirit who yet have failed to incorporate in their moral make-up the virtues of honesty, generosity, courage, and loyalty essential to true and noble living. Some people, it has been said, present the appearance of having been starched before they have been thoroughly washed. [33]

[33] *How Jesus Dealt with Men,* p. 68.

But now in the third place, if keeping our theology in closer touch with morality would make our religion more real to us as individuals, and more socially effective, it follows that our religion would then become more like the religion of Jesus. For surely those were valid marks of his religion. There is no separating Jesus' ethic from his faith. The symbol of his life is a cross, and the cross illumines both his love for God and for man, his devotion to the will of God and his concern for the ethical issues that thwart God's righteous will. His cross therefore gives perennial meaning to his petition that God's will be done on earth as it is in heaven. It must never be forgotten that the cross of Jesus, from which the deepest theological insights of the church have come, rests solidly on the bedrock of moral reality. In going to Calvary Jesus did not by-pass Sinai. The cross would not have been erected if he had. On the contrary he went to his cross precisely because he met the moral and ethical issues of his day squarely and uncompromisingly. This aroused the opposition of his bitterest enemies, the Pharisees and the Sadducees.

It was not a disagreement about religion as such that kindled their opposition. It was rather Jesus' exposé of their lack of moral earnestness that evoked their bitter hostility. The Pharisees were offended because Jesus decried the hollowness of a piety which, while outwardly pretentious, yet lacked inner moral integrity. The Sadducees were aroused because he attacked the shady unethical dealings which converted the Father's house into a den of thieves. We may justly say therefore that it was Jesus' insistence that theology

81

be made morally and ethically meaningful that was directly responsible for his crucifixion.

How can we allow his cross to become so often a symbol that stirs the emotion but fails to arouse the will? It is one of the ironies of history that Christians can on the one hand become so deeply moved by the fact of Jesus' death, and on the other be so seemingly indifferent to the moral and ethical values for which he died. It is an astounding fact that we can work out such an elaborate theology of the cross and yet evade the very moral issues but for his fearless facing of which there probably would have been no cross at all. In so far as we are guilty of this we make the preaching of the gospel of no effect; in fact we are not preaching the gospel of Jesus. "A Christianity that worships Christ emotionally but does not follow him morally is a conventional sham, and too much of our ecclesiastical Christianity today is precisely that." [34]

In the cross then lies the salvation not only of the world but of the church. For the cross is on the one hand a symbol of the most thoroughgoing moral and ethical pioneering the world has known, and on the other an equally unparalleled expression of adventurous faith. Every moral and ethical issue that confronts modern man was met by the Master. Racial bigotry, economic evils, social irresponsibility, international tensions, war—cold or hot. There is no moral problem today which was not in principle faced by this Man who steadfastly set his face to go to Jerusalem, and in going settled once and for all that the Christian religion is irrevocably committed to the ethical issues of life.

[34] Harry Emerson Fosdick, *Riverside Church Monthly*, January, 1931, p .46.

On the other hand the cross is as truly an unequaled symbol of the Christian faith. Indeed more so. For Jesus' faith preceded his ethic. The ethical teachings of Jesus are the fruit of his spiritual pioneering. It was because of what he believed about God that he dared to teach what he did about man in all his relationships, personal and social. Here in the cross is vicarious love in its highest expression. Here is redemption, forgiveness, and grace abounding. This means that the Christian religion is irrevocably committed to a theology, a doctrine of God, who through Christ has spoken his reconciling word for the salvation of the world. In the cross therefore moral reality and theology are one and inseparable. To separate them is on the one hand to reduce Christianity to ethics—a glorified sociology—which Christianity most certainly is not, or on the other to make it a series of theoretical propositions, a dialectic, imposing in the abstract but irrelevant to the burning issues of life. And that is a caricature of the Christian faith.

Christianity is more than morality. It is not less.

III

WAYS OF KNOWING THE TRUTH

IN speaking of ways of knowing the truth we are following an oft-traveled and hence familiar road. However, in view of the line of thought we are developing, it seemed unwise to make a detour. Strictly speaking, we shall not consider the problem of epistemology. The relationship of the knowing mind to the known world presents an interesting and important field of study. It involves the work of such thinkers as Descartes, the English empiricists Locke, Hume, and Berkeley, the work of Kant, and others. But, as I have said, this book's approach to truth is primarily from the viewpoint of Christian faith rather than that of philosophic theories.

One difficulty in the quest of truth is that of mistaking a thoroughfare for a terminus. Sometimes we think we have arrived at the truth when we are actually still on the road to it. We may conscientiously think we have found the truth, but there is often a big difference between what we believe the truth to be and what the truth really is—between our idea of reality and reality itself. Whatever we believe to be true is truth for us, but *our* truth may not be *the* truth. "The most direct source of confusion is that between 'truth for me' and actual or objective truth." [1] This is so because the discovery of truth is gradual or progressive. Truth does not come as with the fullness of light into a darkened room when one turns on a switch. It comes rather like the breaking dawn, at first but dimly seen upon the distant horizon but gradually becoming more luminous, shining "more and more unto the perfect day" (Prov. 4:18).

This of course is understandable. For man's grasp of truth depends so largely upon his fitness, intellectual or spiritual, to receive it. The Master clearly taught this, as when he said to his disciples: "I have yet many things to say unto you, but ye cannot bear them now. Howbeit when he, the Spirit of truth, is come, he will guide you into all truth, . . . and he will show you things to come." (John 16:12-13.) A child does not have the comprehension of a mature person, and there is a childhood of the race no less than of the individual. "We see through a glass, darkly." (I Cor. 13:12.) Sometimes, however, through the increase of knowledge, experience, or faith, the glass becomes clearer and our view of reality more complete. Our unwillingness or inability to see this is a source of endless confusion and trouble. It means that quite often "our" truth becomes the enemy of truth. This can be avoided only as we understand that what is true for one age or generation, the fuller knowledge or more enlightened experience of some other may show to have been only partly true or wholly false. Illustrations of this are found in all areas of life. Science furnishes many. As a little jingle has it:

[1] Arthur Kenyon Rogers, *What Is Truth?* p. 5.

We thought that lines were straight and Euclid true,
God said, "Let Einstein be," and all's askew.[2]

What is askew, however, is not truth, which is unchanged and unchanging, but man's erroneous or incomplete conception of it. The trouble lies not in what is sought but in the limitations of the seeker.

When we say that man progressively discovers truth we do not mean to infer that he is always seeking but never finding. We mean rather that his findings, especially if they are genuine, need not fear the most relentless scrutiny. The one thing truth does not fear is light. We need not hesitate therefore to submit the truth we have found or accepted to any fuller illumination we may receive. I feel certain, however, that some moderns mistake hallucination for illumination. Paul warned about those who were "ever learning, and never able to come to the knowledge of the truth" (II Tim. 3:7). From a Christian point of view that position is untenable. We believe truth can be found—has been found. Said the Master: "Ye shall know the truth" (John 8:32).

How do we know it? Mainly in five ways: authority, reason, intuition, experiment, revelation. To try to discuss these five approaches to reality in one chapter reminds me of the story of the little girl who chose as the subject of her short essay, "The Universe and Other Things"! Yet it may be more satisfactory to open several doors than to explore any one approach more in detail. As it is, I shall devote most of my comments to revelation, since this is the uniquely religious way of knowing

[2] Quoted by Lynn Harold Hough, *The Church and Civilization*, p. 47.

the truth. The other four ways mentioned I shall discuss as succinctly as I am able.

First, authority; notice, not authoritarianism. Fortunately or unfortunately thoroughgoing authoritarianism is not available for Protestants. It is, however, the method par excellence of Roman Catholics. They are taught to believe that the Roman church has a monopoly on Christian truth and is its sole God-appointed custodian and interpreter. A manual of Catholic theology teaches that faith is "assent on authority, that is to say, the acceptance of a proposition, not because we ourselves perceive its truth, but because another person tells us that it is true." [3] Said the Master: "Seek, and ye shall find" (Matt. 7:7). The Roman Catholic does not seek; he accepts. His duty is to take, simply and unquestioningly, what someone else has allegedly found.

Father George Tyrrell voiced perfectly the Roman Catholic position:

In all my life, . . . now fully forty-seven years, I cannot remember a single temptation against faith that seemed to me to have any force. The church's teaching is before me, as a glorious series of splendid certainties. My mind is absolutely satisfied, . . . I have no private judgment to overcome, and no desire to exercise my private judgment. It is a greater pleasure to receive and possess truth with certainty, than to go in search of it and to be in uncertainty whether it has been found.[4]

This sort of authoritarianism deprives one of the enriching, though at times disturbing, experiences that are part of the

---

[3] Quoted by Harris Franklin Rall, *Christianity,* p. 213.
[4] *Autobiography,* p. 229.

quest. To be wholly spared the intellectual and moral disciplines encumbent on those who seek is to remain among the spiritually immature.

To say that the genius of Protestantism is away from authoritarianism is not to say, however, that Protestantism is devoid of authority. Unlike the scribes, Jesus was not an authoritarian but spoke "as one having authority" (Matt 7:29). His authority was not external, legal or official, but moral and spiritual. It sprang from the intrinsic nature of the truth he taught and exemplified. His was the authority of truth. "Master, we know that thou art true, and teachest the way of God in truth." (Matt. 22:16.) How did they know? Because they sensed about him that which was so obviously genuine.

> For truth has such a face and such a mien,
> As to be lov'd needs only to be seen.[5]

That is to say, there is a self-evidencing quality in truth, and the Master possessed it in fullest measure.

While therefore Protestants cannot accept authoritarianism as a road to truth, and have good reason to think that such a road misleads more often than it leads, it would be wholly wrong to suppose that authority plays no part in the Protestant's discovery of truth. It does. The church suggests such authority. Though humanly errant it is a divinely inspired institution. It is not authoritative in its own right, above criticism, correction, or corruption; or in a position to command by decree or convince by dogma. It may not therefore be

---

[5] Dryden, *The Hind and the Panther.*

regarded as omniscient or infallible. It is but as an earthern vessel, yet it is God's earthern vessel, custodian of the treasure of his revelation. Through its blessed fellowship and the high privilege of re-creating and enriching worship, God has spoken, and speaks, to the soul of man.

The Bible speaks to us with authority. We may not regard it as an inerrant book, "every word true from cover to cover," as though God intended it to be an infallible guide upon all subjects. The founder of Protestantism did not so regard it. Luther daringly said that the Bible was not the Word of God but that it *contained* the Word of God. This is another way of saying that for the Protestant, authority is not in the Bible as an external guide but in the Bible as its truths are made reasonable and real to the enlightened conscience of the individual Christian. In Protestantism the ultimate authority is not external but inward. It lies in the human soul as it is illumined by God's spirit. The far-reaching implications of this fact Protestants are loath to accept. Applying this concept of authority to the Bible, however, far from lessening its significance, immeasurably enhances it. For it puts the Bible in the area of human life and experience, out of which it came and in which its divine insights were molded. This is why time only confirms and establishes the imperishable truths of this incomparable lamp to our feet and light to our path, whose authority is "the spiritual authority of luminous and compelling insight."

The lives of saintly souls, the living epistles, "sons of God, . . . in the midst of a crooked and perverse nation," who "shine as lights in the world; holding forth the word of life" (Phil.

2:15-16), speak with the authority of truth. There are truths established through generations of Christian life and experience that we simply cannot brush aside without being spiritually impoverished. The modern does not scientifically speaking start *de novo*, as though nothing had been proved in the scientific realm. No more need the modern, morally or ethically speaking, start that way. Just as one proceeds scientifically in the light of the failures and findings of his predecessors, and does not knowingly repeat their mistakes, but avoids the dead-end streets as he follows their proved and tested leads to reality, so may one in the vastly more important realm of spiritual reality. It is simply preposterous to suppose that while we can hold to well-established truths in the scientific realm, we are all at sea in the moral realm. To think that nineteen hundred years of Christian life and experience have left no valid guides for the modern pilgrim on his way, is the height of folly. Only the fool thinks that, morally speaking, wisdom was born with him. If, as the prodigal of old, we feel it incumbent upon us to find out for ourselves what the far country is like, we shall indeed find out. Our discovery, however, will not add any new insight to the moral topography of that territory. We shall only discover again that "the wages of sin is death," a truth that has been verified often enough. In our "adventure" we shall be as "original" as one who leaps from a roof to find out firsthand whether the law of gravity works. It does!

The authority of Protestantism is therefore not official, external, or legal. It is the authority of experience as it comes to us through worship, the Bible, and the lives of men who have tasted and seen how gracious the Lord is, and whose experiences remain as guideposts on our way.

Another road to truth is reason. There are some who maintain that it is the only valid road, and others who, as far as the Christian faith is concerned, would think very lightly of it, if indeed they would not discredit it altogether. It is difficult to see how we could discard reason. True to the tradition of his fathers the Master taught: "Thou shalt love the Lord thy God with all thy . . . mind" (Matt. 22:37). God has revealed himself through his word, his logos, his reason. The mind's love of truth must not be regarded as being at daggers drawn with the heart's love of God. Of course there has often been hostility between reason and faith. Tertullian asked indignantly: "What indeed has Athens to do with Jerusalem?" Luther said: "The whole of Aristotle is to theology as darkness is to light." To those who say "Nobody becomes a theologian without Artistotle," Luther answers: "Quite the reverse: only without Aristotle can we become theologians." [6] The Middle Ages were singularly free of the conflict between rationalism and Christianity because by and large during that period the rationalists were themselves the theologians. The antagonism between reason and religion is the fruit of the Renaissance, which so exalted reason as to give it monopolistic rights over truth. So Hegel wrote: "While the Gates of Hell were never able to prevail against the Christian Church, the Gates of Reason have."

Of course the gates of reason have not done anything of the kind. To say that they have is, as William Temple put it,

[6] Étienne Gilson, *Reason and Revelation in the Middle Ages*, pp. 9, 93-94.

"the heresy of intellectualism." This heresy fails to distinguish between the reasonable and the rationalistic. It is based on the assumption that nothing can be known rationally unless it be scientifically known. Now the deepest truth of Christianity is not rationalistic, but most certainly it is reasonable. To say that it is not is, as Paul Tillich argues, to miss the broader implications of reason as "the very principle of humanity" and to reduce it to "technical reason." But reason cannot be regarded in so limited a sense unless we decide arbitrarily to write off what are by all odds the most significant and meaningful aspects of reality. It is impossible to identify the real with the concrete. As George Santayana puts it: "Whoever it was who searched the heavens with a telescope and found no God would not have found the human mind if he had searched the brain with a microscope." [7]

It should be evident to anyone that a purely intellectual approach to reality is always a partial approach. As H. S. Jennings, the great biologist, wrote: "It is the Nemesis of the struggle for exactitude by the man of science that leads him to present a mutilated, merely fractional account of the world as a true and complete picture." [8] Intellectually all water is H_2O. From the viewpoint of "technical reason" not only is the mud puddle H_2O, but so also is the mountainous wave lashed up by a storm at sea. So also is awe-inspiring Niagara, Mirror Lake in Yosemite reflecting mountains and sky, or Lake Louise nestled in the Canadian Rockies. From a purely intellectual approach the dirty little mud puddle that plays havoc with

[7] Quoted by L. P. Jacks, *The Confession of an Octogenarian*, p. 176.
[8] *American Scientist*, January, 1948, p. 133.

your "shine" is on a par with all the rest of them. It too is H_2O.
But is that the end of the matter? Intellectually it may be. But
life contradicts such a verdict. As Harry Emerson Fosdick once
graphically wrote: "For the purposes of his science, the nerves of
a frog and the nerves of a Michelangelo, the brain of a newt
and of a Newton would be equally objects of his regard. They
are all biological tissue." [9] But surely the purposes of science,
mechanical, technical, highly selective and specialized as they
are, are by no manner of means wide or vast enough to encompass the purposes of life. Is Shakespeare's *Hamlet* meaningless
because we cannot extract the cube root of it? As Hartley Burr
Alexander says: "The net of reason is too loose of mesh if all the
shining things escape it." [10] What would a purely intellectual
or technical appraisal of a friend yield in terms of friendship?
It would be as far removed from the rich values of friendship
as an X-ray picture of a loved one would be from the loved one
himself. G. K. Chesterton may have been right after all when he
said: "A lunatic is not a man who has lost his reason; he is a
man who has lost everything except his reason." [11]

It is reassuring to know that some scientists are coming to see
this. One of them writes:

In the past, we scientists have gone into the laboratory to find
truth. And, as we entered, we closed the door behind us to shut
out the world of men. Never again will we do that. If we are to
find truth, that door must be open. There is no truth in a laboratory

[9] *Adventurous Religion*, p. 171.
[10] *Truth and the Faith*, p. 272.
[11] Quoted by L. P. Jacks, *op. cit.*, p. 78.

which has cut itself off from communication with the human living.[12]

Such thinkers are coming to realize that a purely intellectual approach to reality, if indeed there is such a thing, no more adequately portrays life than does a human skeleton the living man. Nonetheless, reason, as far as it goes, is a valid road to truth.

A third way of knowing the truth is that of intuition or insight. "Truth not only reasons with Aristotle, but sometimes sings with Homer." [13] Intuition is the realm of feeling but it must not be confused with instinct. Its roots are not simply biological. There is that about intuition which is akin to perception. Intuition is insight, not instinct. It is cognitive. The knowledge thus gained cannot of course be as precise or exact as that of the reason. Socrates well described this kind of knowledge when he said: "I cannot indeed be confident that this is the exact truth, but that something like this is the truth I am confident."

Kant laid the basis for intuitionism by distinguishing between what he called the pure or speculative reason as opposed to the practical reason. He taught that the pure reason cannot know ultimate reality. It knows only the phenomenal world—the world of sense perception. It is by the practical reason that one knows ultimate truth, the truth of what he called the "noumenal" world. Of course, strictly speaking, Kant does not admit any *knowledge* of ultimate truth whatsoever. But it is our right and duty to make certain great *postulates* concerning ultimate re-

[12] Quoted by Alexander Meiklejohn, *New York Times Magazine*, August, 11, 1946, p. 48.
[13] Jay William Hudson, *The Truths We Live By*, p. 113.

ality (like God, freedom, and immortality), since they are rationally required if doing the right is to be a reasonable act. Nevertheless, as I have said, his distinction between the pure reason as opposed to the practical reason laid the basis for intuitionism, which Bergson defines as "the kind of intellectual sympathy by which one places oneself within an object in order to coincide with what is unique in it and consequently inexpressible." [14]

A good example of how intuition works is found in an amusing anecdote from Chinese lore. It happened that Chuang Tzu and Hui Tzu had strolled onto a bridge over the river Hao, when the former observed: "See how the minnows are darting about! That is the pleasure of fishes."

"You not being a fish yourself," said Hui Tzu, "how can you possibly know in what consists the pleasure of fishes?"

"And you not being I," retorted Chuang, "how can you know that I do not know?"

"If I, not being you, cannot know what you know," urged Hui Tzu, "it follows that you, not being a fish, cannot know in what consists the pleasure of fishes."

"Let us go back," said Chuang Tzu, "to your original question. You asked me *how* I knew in what consists the pleasure of fishes. Your very question shows that you knew I knew. I knew it from my own feelings on this bridge." [15]

Now there are three features of this quaint yet profound anecdote that should be noticed because they reveal three

[14] D. Miall Edwards, *The Philosophy of Religion*, p. 190.
[15] Milton G. Evans, "Religious Realism," *Crozer Quarterly*, January, 1932, pp. 33-34.

characteristic features of the knowledge that comes through intuition. For one thing, intuition is the response of the total personality. In approaching the scene from the bridge by reason the mind would be the primary or sole observer. Intuitively our whole self responds. Then again, whereas intellectually or scientifically we should catch one minnow and analyze or dissect it, intuitively the whole scene is brought within our view. Finally, by the way of reason, the conclusion would be reached after prolonged study or investigation, while intuitively there is an *immediacy* to our knowledge. So the knowledge of truth that comes by intuition is that of the whole personality—mind, heart, and imagination—responding to a total situation, and gaining some immediate impression.

Those who are wont to question the validity of intuition as a road to reality may find it hard to explain how even in the field of science intuition plays so large a role. Many scientific discoveries have come as flashes of insight. Though familiar, let us recall a few. Archimedes, in a flash of insight, discovered the principle of hydrostatics; so did Newton the principle of gravitation by observing a falling apple. Galileo discovered the law of oscillation of the pendulum by watching the movement of the chandeliers in the cathedral at Pisa. In like manner did Robert Mayer the law of the mechanical equivalence of heat from a chance happening on a voyage. The case of Henri Poincaré is also worthy of note. He had been unsuccessfully working on a mathematical problem. He put it from his mind. One day, walking on a cliff overlooking the sea, the mathematical idea he had sought came to him with the "characteristics of conciseness, suddenness, and immediate certainty." So to these and similar searchers after truth, doors that could not be opened by labored and painstaking effort yielded instantly to the touch of insight or intuition.

It is, however, in the field of religion that intuition is most operative. The great truths of Christianity are not the result of labored argument. It is astonishing how little argument there is in the Bible, and how much truth. Or maybe it would be astonishing were it otherwise! For the winning of an argument does not necessarily mean the discovery of truth. That God is never found at the end of an argument is a familiar observation. I must point out, however, that even as the scientific insights mentioned above came, not just to anybody, but only to those who were scientifically prepared, so too the great Christian insights are grasped only by those who are spiritually prepared. The natural man receives not the things of science; they must be scientifically discerned. No more does the natural man receive the things of the spirit; they must, as Paul says, be spiritually discerned. When Pothinus, bishop of Lyons, in the heroic age of the Christian religion, was dragged before the Roman governor and asked, "Who is the god of the Christians?" he replied, "If thou art worthy, thou shalt know."

Just so! Only to those who meet the requirements, who are prepared, does God send his insights. The preparation required for the apprehension of spiritual truth is not technical, else God could speak only to the learned; rather it is a kind of preparation open to all. The requirements are moral and spiritual—singleness of heart and purpose. "Blessed are the pure in heart: for they shall see God." (Matt. 5:8.) "The meek will he guide in judgment: and the meek will he teach his way." (Ps. 25:9.) A simple soul surrendered to God, and sincerely trying to do his righteous will, is vastly more likely to grasp spiritual truth than the most learned of arrogant or haughty mein. "I praise thee, Father, Lord of heaven and earth, for hiding all this from the wise and learned and revealing it to the simpleminded." (Matt. 11:25 Moffatt.) The poet may well have been thinking of the spiritually prepared when he wrote:

It is they
Who utter wisdom from the central deep,
And, listening to the inner flow of things,
Speak to the age out of eternity.[16]

A fourth way of knowing the truth is that of experiment. "If any man will do his will, he shall know." (John 7:17.) Stanley Jones was right when he said that it is easier to act your way into right thinking than to think your way into right acting. As William Adams Brown has said: "God is the subject of experiment in religion in the same sense in which nature is the subject of experiment in science." [17]

Why is it that in the Christian religion doing leads to knowing? Let me suggest two reasons. For one thing our willingness to act indicates that we are sincere. Christian truth is not likely to be grasped by the spiritual dilettante but is apprehended only by those who are morally in earnest. As Pascal said: "Human things must be known in order to be loved, but divine things must be loved in order to be known." In 1851 Robertson of Brighton preached a sermon on the subject "Obedience, the

[16] James Russell Lowell, "Columbus."
[17] Pathways to Certainty, p. 210.

Organ of Spiritual Knowledge." Without this attitude much of our religious discussion is unilluminating and ineffectual. We sometimes talk about religion as we do about the weather, with not the slightest intention of doing anything about it. But we can and must do something about Christianity if we are to know its truth. That youth who came to his old minister, allegedly disturbed about certain discrepancies in the Bible, probably deserved the rebuke of the old man who said to him: "Young man, never mind about the mistakes of Moses. Where were you last night?" Too often, like this youth, we are intellectually curious but not morally serious. In the Christian religion that attitude gets us precisely nowhere.

We frequently quote the words of Jesus: "Ye shall know the truth, and the truth shall make you free" (John 8:32). We are quite wrong, however, in separating those words from what precedes them. The whole text, as you recall, is: "If ye continue in my word, then are ye my disciples indeed; and ye shall know the truth, and the truth shall make you free" (John 8:31-32). "If ye continue in my word"—that is the requirement to be met. It is not met just by talking about the truth but by striving to live it. To say this is not, of course, to minimize either the necessity or importance of religious discussion. Rather is it to say that discussion is of value when it clarifies the issue and leads to action. We can no more arrive at Christian truth by the discussion route alone than can the church, gathered in convention, transform society by passing resolutions about social evils and letting it go at that.

We know by doing, then, because moral seriousness is indispensable to the apprehension of Christian truth. Jesus, when he called his disciples, did not begin by asking them what they believed. He demanded no creedal statement as a prerequisite to discipleship. It was not until near the end of his public ministry at Caesarea Philippi that he asked: "But who say ye that I am?" (Matt. 16:15.) The basic requirement was their moral earnestness: "Follow me"; "Come unto me"; "Learn of me." They would learn as they followed; there was no other way. Wrote Paul: "I follow after, . . . that I may apprehend that for which also I am apprehended of Christ Jesus." (Phil. 3:12.) Renan, a great admirer of Pasteur, once gave the French chemist the following mild admonition:

Truth, Sir, is a great coquette; she will not be sought with too much passion, but often is most amenable to indifference. She escapes when apparently caught, but gives herself up if patiently waited for; revealing herself after farewells have been said, but inexorable when loved with too much fervor.[18]

No doubt we may seek truth so passionately as to mistake our enthusiasm for reality. But for every person who loses truth from overzealous persistence, one hundred miss her from lack of moral seriousness.

But in the apprehension of Christian truth, doing is a path to knowing not only because it is an indication of our sincerity but also because there is that in the very nature of Christianity which calls for action if its truth is to be known. It is not without significance that the Master connected truth with "way" and "life." "I am the way, the truth, and the life." (John 14:6.) Americans are often accused by Europeans of being activists

[18] Quoted by Paul DeKruif, *Microbe Hunters*, p. 169.

100

in religion. Is there not a sense in which the charge can be leveled against Christianity itself? Christianity by its very nature is activist. The Golden Rule is not a passive rule of conduct, nor are such commands as: "Follow me," "Learn of me," "Go ye." The verbs are all active. "Why call ye me Lord, Lord, and do not the things that I say?" (Luke 6:46.) In the final judgment the test was not one of right thinking merely, but of right thinking resulting in right acting. "Inasmuch as ye have done it unto one of the least of these." (Matt. 25:40.)

The emphasis on action appears too in the symbols by which Jesus describes his kingdom: bread, water, salt, light, seed, leaven, coins, and so on. These are not objects of abstract contemplation, they are involved in the whole business of living. So too the individuals whom Jesus mentions most frequently. Who are they? Farmers, carpenters, shepherds, fishermen, bakers, bankers, dressmakers, merchants, travelers—all people of action. This does not mean that Christianity has no room for contemplation—far from that—for like Martha we can be careful and troubled about so many things as to miss the one thing needful. It means only that Christian truth is made known not in abstract thinking about life, but in being deeply involved in the living of life. "Wist ye not that I must be about my Father's business?" (Luke 2:49.) That business was so intimately related to the affairs of this world that it brought Jesus into conflict with the powers that be and led to his crucifixion.

The great truths of our religion, like "the supplication of a righteous man," are made known "in its working" (Jas. 5:16 A.S.V.). "Lord, teach us to pray." (Luke 11:1.) We would probably have said: "Lord, tell us about prayer. Give us a lecture on the subject." In apparent contradiction to what we have been saying about American activism, Europeans tell this story on us. They say no American will ever get to heaven because on the way to the celestial city one comes at length to a finger post. The arm on the right is marked "To Heaven," the one on the left reads "To Lectures About Heaven." Americans all turn left! It is significant that the disciples did not want to know about prayer, but *how* to pray. Their approach was not theoretical but practical. Many of us find it much easier to read books about prayer than through discipline to learn the art of prayer. So with all Christian truth. Yet only as we forgive do we come to know the Christian meaning of forgiveness. Christian brotherhood is understood only as we are brotherly. "And who is my neighbor?" (Luke 10:29.) The answer was not a dissertation on "The Sociological Significance of Neighborliness and Its Bearing on Our Religious Traditions." It was a story illuminating an *act* of neighborliness, and concluding with: "Go, and *do* thou likewise" (Luke 10:37). "If any man will do his will, he shall know." (John 7:17.)

Is it not by this method that we have come to know the greatest of all truths, the truth about God? The God we worship did not come from Greece, where the sophisticated were always anxious to tell and hear some new thing. He was not the God of philosophy, who is approached by logical argument. Our God came from Palestine. He was the God not of speculation but of religious experience—the God who revealed himself in the struggles and disciplines of a people who in great faith lived as though God were their Father and Ruler. Writes Eugene W. Lyman:

Experimental faithfulness . . . is not a blind faithfulness, but one based on abundant knowledge; but it is experimental faithfulness because it fulfills conditions essential to further knowledge. Without the "firm belief" carried out into action the fuller possibilities . . . cannot be known.[19]

Someday, perchance, we shall see, as has often been suggested, that our primary duty is not to explain religious experience but to realize that it is the explanation regal over all.

These four ways of knowing the truth that we have mentioned must not be regarded as operating wholly independently of each other. They complement and supplement one another. Authority and insight may be regarded as pathfinders on the way to truth, reason and experiment confirmers; reason and experiment keep authority and insight from soaring out of sight —they correct any excesses or overemphases we may be wont to indulge. These four ways therefore overlap and are interrelated.

Now let us discuss revelation. This is the uniquely religious way of knowing the truth. I do not say uniquely Christian, for "belief in revelation, in one form or another, seems to be characteristic of all religion." [20] It is, however, the uniquely religious way.

How shall we think of revelation? Must we regard it as a completely separate and distinct way of knowing, or can we say that the truth that comes through authority, reason, insight, and experiment is in a real sense a revelation of God?

[19] *The Meaning and Truth of Religion,* p. 164.
[20] H. H. Farmer, *The World and God,* p. 77.

Some thinkers so maintain. "Even reason," writes one of my former teachers, William Adams Brown, "the way of all ways that is most often set over against revelation as man's way in contrast to God's, is recognized . . . as a form, even though a lower form, of revelation." [21] At the other extreme would be a theologian like Karl Barth, to whom revelation is limited exclusively to one specific act in history—the cross and resurrection of Christ—and has no further meaning for religion. To be sure, Barth would agree that there are other indications of God's working in history. But he refers to them as "tokens." Revelation is through Christ alone. I suppose the position of most of us would be somewhere in between. While we would not confine the word revelation solely to God's intervention in Christ, we would maintain that in its biblical sense revelation suggests a type of knowledge that can be obtained in no other way except as it pleases God to disclose it.

This idea is not too popular. The popular word with us is "discovery." The way to truth, we like to think, is a one-way street. The only truth we ever know is that which we ourselves discover, and eventually we shall discover all there is. Historic Christianity, on the contrary, while it admonishes us to seek, assures us that we are being sought. In our quest for truth we are like men tunneling a mountain—there is activity at both ends. As we try to discover the truth, God seeks to reveal it to us.

> Think you mid all this mighty sum
> Of things forever speaking,

[21] *Pathways to Certainty*, p. 78.

104

That nothing of itself will come,
But we must still be seeking? [22]

Let us consider revelation from two approaches. First, why we believe in it, and second, where we find evidences of it. Why do we believe that God reveals himself? Our faith in revelation rests upon two assumptions. The first is that finite man cannot of himself discover the ultimate truth; the second, that truth is by its very nature communicative. Let us proceed now to discuss these two assumptions.

That there is a truth which lies beyond the power of man fully to comprehend seems undeniable. What the mind has discovered is amazing, but what man does not know, and in the nature of the case cannot fathom, is even more astonishing. As Thomas Edison puts it: "No one knows one seven-billionth of one per cent about anything." Whether or not his percentage is right is for our purposes unimportant. The important fact is that after knowledge has taken us as far as it can, we stand before a closed door. Far from solving all mysteries, the increase of knowledge has increased the field of the unknown and deepened the mystery of life. Tennyson put it well:

For Knowledge is the swallow on the lake
That sees and stirs the surface-shadow there
But never yet hath dipt into the abysm. [23]

It may be salutary to hear the verdict of several scientific men on this question. Here is Ernst Haeckel:

[22] Wordsworth, "Expostulation and Reply."
[23] Tennyson, "The Ancient Sage."

We grant at once that the innermost character of nature is just as little understood by us as it was by Anaximander and Empedocles twenty-four hundred years ago. . . . We must even grant that this essence and substance become more mysterious and enigmatic the deeper we penetrate into the knowledge of its attributes.[24]

Or listen to Arthur Eddington, who concludes a series of lectures by saying:

I should have liked to have closed these lectures by leading up to some great climax. But perhaps it is more in accordance with the true conditions of scientific progress that they should fizzle out with a glimpse of the obscurity which marks the frontiers of present knowledge.[25]

John Burroughs expressed the same idea. He writes: "We have in our hands a rope with only one end. In trying to find the other end, we only get ourselves hopelessly tied up." [26] These are but a few of many views which reiterate the limitations of human knowledge. Revelation, then, rests on the assumption that when the mind "fizzles out" in obscurity God reveals the truth to man; that as man comes to the end of his rope God puts a solid rock beneath his feet. Or, as Paul once put it: "But we speak the wisdom of God in a mystery, even the hidden wisdom, . . . which none of the princes of this world knew. . . . But God hath revealed them unto us by his Spirit: for the Spirit searcheth all things, yea, the deep things of God." (I Cor.

[24] Quoted by Harry Emerson Fosdick, *Adventurous Religion*, p. 155.
[25] Quoted by Walter Lippmann, *A Preface to Morals*, p. 126.
[26] *Accepting the Universe*, p. 282.

2:7-8, 10.) So you see, what man does not know, and in the nature of the case cannot, God reveals. That is our faith.

Does this faith seem unreasonable? In trying to answer this question let us ask another: "Has science discovered God?" This is a quite natural question for a scientifically-minded age to ask. Science has discovered so much, why not God? Science indeed has discovered a power, an intelligence, in and behind nature. "Seven Reasons Why a Scientist Believes in God" is the title of a magazine article.[27] But to know that there is a power in the universe is not enough. We must know the nature of this power. Is this "god" personal or impersonal, good, bad or indifferent, weak or strong, wise or foolish? Science cannot answer that question. The character of ultimate reality lies beyond the mind of man to comprehend. In this sense the answer to the age-old question "Canst thou by searching find out God?" (Job 11:7), is "No." This is why faith in revelation is an essential ingredient of all religion. For the religious life cannot be nurtured on the mere assurance that "God" is. It must know *who* or *what* God is—the nature of the ultimately real—"The only begotten Son . . . he hath declared him" (John 1:18). Such is our faith.

Should it seem strange that the answer to the question "Has science discovered God?" is a negative one, then let us ask a simpler question: "Has science discovered man?" The answer to that too is "No." To be sure science has discovered a great deal about man—biological and phychological—yet the deepest truth about man, which is neither biological nor psychological but moral and spiritual, science cannot discover. For

[27] *Reader's Digest,* December, 1946.

Man hath all that Nature hath, but *more,*
And in that more lie all his hopes of good.[28]

It is that "more" which transcends nature and sense perception, and therefore transcends science, that knowledge cannot
fathom.

The truth of this statement appears as we consider how those
who stand solely on the plane of nature describe man. "What
is man?" asks the psalmist. Nietzsche, standing on the plane of
nature, replies: "The earth has a skin. That skin is full of sores.
One of these sores is called man." Haeckel, in a similar vein,
writes: "Our human nature . . . sinks [under scientific scrutiny]
to the level of a placental mammal, which has no more value for
the universe at large than an ant, or the fly of a summer's day,
. . . or the smallest bacillus."

But Christianity has a different idea about man: "Beloved,
now are we the sons of God, and it doth not yet appear what
we shall be: but we know that, when he shall appear, we shall
be like him; for we shall see him as he is." (I John 3:2.) "This
mortal must put on immortality." (I Cor. 15:53.) That position
was not reached by man's unaided mind. Flesh and blood have
not revealed that unto us. It is a part of the heritage of Christian faith. It passes knowledge. Revelation therefore rests on
the assumption that what the mind cannot discover God has
revealed or will reveal.

There is, however, another assumption that lies behind the
idea of revelation—not only that the mind cannot discover
the ultimate truth but also that truth is by its nature communi-

[28] A. E. Taylor, *Faith of a Moralist,* p. 119.

cative. This communicative quality is the mark of all truth. When a scientist works with nature it is not as though he were excavating the tomb of some Egyptian mummy. For nature is no mummy. Nature is alive. If the universe were like a corpse, "dumb and inarticulate," it is incredible that man could have made such progress in science as he has. Actually when he knocks at the right door he does not have to knock it down— the door swings open. When he finds the right formula nature responds. If we plough and plant we reap—nature responds.

If this quality of responsiveness obtains in inanimate nature, how much more in personality. However much more than personal the Christian God may be, Christian faith maintains he is not less than personal. For it is impossible to conceive how a being who was less than personal could have created personality. Can a stream rise higher than its source? Now personal truth, by which I mean truth incarnate in personality, is par excellence communicative truth. No wonder, then, that one bedrock Christian conviction is that God seeks us even as we seek him, that as we are trying to discover him he seeks to reveal himself to us. "He made known his ways unto Moses, his acts unto the children of Israel." (Ps. 103:7.) Moses did not have to find it all out by himself. Indeed in the Christian tradition we go further and claim not only that man's search for God is a double search, but that the initiative in the search is with God.

> He moved my soul to seek Him, seeking me;
> It was not I that found, O Saviour true—
> No, I was found of Thee.[29]

[29] From the anonymous hymn "I Sought the Lord."

As John Baillie has said: "To our human activity of faith there has always seemed to correspond a divine activity of *grace;* and to our human activity of discovery a divine activity of self-disclosure." [30] To the question, then, "Why do we believe in revelation?" we answer, "Because we cannot of ourselves discover the ultimate truth, and because truth is by its nature communicative."

But we must ask not only "Why does God reveal himself?" but, "Where does he reveal himself?" Confining ourselves to the Judaic-Christian tradition we mention three avenues. First, in the external world—in nature. "The heavens declare the glory of God" (Ps. 19:1), or as Paul says: "For the invisible things of him since the creation . . . are clearly seen, being perceived through the things that are made, even his ever-lasting power and divinity" (Rom. 1:20 A.S.V.). Primitive peoples did not speak of seeing God in nature; they identified God with nature. Nature did not reveal God—it was God. This point of view, however, is not found in the Bible, either in the Old or the New Testament. The Jews were never pantheistic. They never identified God with nature. Rather, they saw nature as the avenue through which God revealed himself. Since the Bible never identifies God with nature, it follows that the Bible does not regard nature as giving a complete picture of God. Job expressed that well: "Lo, these are parts of his ways: but how little a portion is heard of him? but the thunder of his power who can understand?" (Job 26:14.) Job is much nearer the Christian point of view than those philosophic naturalists

[30] *Interpretation of Religion,* p. 448.

like Francis Bacon, for example, who taught that nature is not a part of his ways but quite exhausts our knowledge of reality. Christianity completely repudiates the claim that "the only road which can lead us to a knowledge of the Creator must be cut through the things of sense." [31]

Men have found God revealed not only in nature but in history. "In the year that King Uzziah died I saw the Lord." (Isa. 6:1.) In this political crisis which had befallen his nation Isaiah saw divine implications.

There are three ways in which God reveals himself in history. First, through the mighty acts: "One generation shall praise thy works to another, and shall declare thy mighty acts. I will speak of the glorious honor of thy majesty, and of thy wondrous works" (Ps. 145:4, 5). What are some of these "mighty acts"? Among them we should surely mention the deliverance of the Israelites from Egypt, the covenant at Sinai, the impact of the prophets, the birth of the Master, the founding of the Christian church. Some might mention such events as the voyage of the Pilgrim Fathers, who, like Abraham of old, "went out, not knowing whither he went" (Heb. 11:8). So at least the poet thought, for he sang:

> O God, beneath thy guiding hand,
> Our exiled fathers crossed the sea.[32]

It is true that those who are contemporary with such events may not see God in them. It often takes the perspective of time to reveal the hand of God in the affairs of men. The

---

[31] Étienne Gilson. *See* John Baillie, *Our Knowledge of God*, p. 129.
[32] Leonard Bacon, "O God, Beneath Thy Guiding Hand."

Israelites as they journeyed complained: "Ye have brought us forth into this wilderness, to kill this whole assembly with hunger" (Exod. 16:3). They longed for the fleshpots of Egypt and wished they had died there. Yet today we have no doubt that the hand of God was in their deliverance. To his contemporaries in general the birth of Jesus, surely a mighty act if ever there was one, was just the birth of another baby. We do not so regard it. Indeed we find it difficult at times to see the hand of God in the events of our own lives as individuals. Sometimes it is not until the individual has passed through some hard, bleak, unsheltered experience that in looking back he can say with Jacob: "Surely the Lord is in this place; and I knew it not" (Gen. 28:16). Perspective therefore is necessary if one is to behold the works of the Lord in his dealing with the corporate group as with the individual.

But God reveals himself in history not only through his mighty acts but also through the operation of his moral laws, within which man must work out his destiny. Here God often appears in judgment. "Behold . . . the goodness and severity of God," writes Paul. (Rom. 11:22.) God is love and his mercy endureth forever, but the love of God is holy love and cannot condone human sin. The tragic experiences of the prodigal in the far country do not indicate a lack of parental love: they only prove the moral trustworthiness of a universe in which we reap what we sow. To go against the grain of a moral universe is to reap a harvest of desolation and destruction. When we flout the eternal principles of truth and justice there is no possible way of escaping the day of judgment.

There is a third way in which God reveals himself in history

—not only through his mighty acts and his moral laws, but through the great personalities of history. "The God of Abraham, of Isaac, and of Jacob." (Exod. 3:16.) Through such men and others like them, Moses, David, Elijah, Jeremiah, people were made aware of God and came to know him. Indeed men like Isaiah, Hosea and Jeremiah spoke of themselves as "'signs'—visible pledges of what God was doing for Israel." [33] It was inevitable that men would come at last to see God revealed through personality. For if Emerson was right when he said that an institution is but the lengthened shadow of a man, then so are historic events the lengthened shadows of men. Moral principles operate through moral personalities. It was therefore natural that men should move from events and principles to persons, in and through whom events and principles become meaningful and operative.

You see, then, how the stage is set for God's greatest intervention in history through the greatest personality of history, Jesus Christ our Lord. That in Christ, God has revealed himself in a unique way is the faith of all Christians. We believe with the unknown author of the Epistle to the Hebrews that God who spoke of old through the prophets has now spoken to us in his Son. This is the great truth of the Incarnation. It bids us believe that in Bethlehem of the long ago something happened that is unique. The God of whom men caught glimpses in the beauty and order of nature, in history-making events, in the moral principles that undergird his universe, in the great personalities that sought his righteous will, revealed

[33] E. F. Scott, *New Testament Idea of Revelation*, p. 44.

himself at last in Christ Jesus, gave forth the "light of the knowledge of the glory of God in the face of Jesus Christ" (II Cor. 4:6), who is "the brightness of his glory, and the express image of his person" (Heb. 1:3).

Here, then, in outline form is the story as to where God reveals himself: in nature through its beauty and order; in history through his mighty acts, his moral principles that undergird the historic process; and in the great personalities that incarnate his truth, culminating in him who is the truth incarnate—Jesus Christ our Lord.

Is this the end of the road to revelation? No, for there is yet another place where God makes himself known to us. In a sense this is the most important of all: within our own hearts, in our moral consciousness, "the still small voice"— within. We seem to be driven back each time to this inner moral truth, moral reality, as by some irresistible logic.

This is the most important because whether or not one sees the truth of revelation anywhere depends upon whether one is inwardly equipped to do so. Take an illustration from the physical world. Modern man inhabits a vastly more wonderful universe than his fathers did, a universe in which what he regards as commonplace would have in other days seemed incredible or miraculous. Why? The answer lies not in nature, where all these secrets have been potentially present, but in man. Science has provided man with the technological equipment for the discovery of truths which were heretofore hidden. The most powerful broadcasting station goes unheard without a receiving set.

Now the inner moral sense, what the Master called "the

light that is in thee" (Matt. 6:23), is the receiving set, so to speak, of the spiritual world. This is why it may be regarded as the most important area of God's revelation. It is the key to all else. Writes Jeremiah:

"This shall be the covenant that I will make with the house of Israel; After those days, saith the Lord, I will put my law in their inward parts, and write it in their hearts; and will be their God, and they shall be my people. And they shall teach no more every man his neighbor, and every man his brother, saying, Know the Lord: for they shall all know me, from the least of them unto the greatest of them, saith the Lord" (Jer. 31:33-34).

So God puts "in our hearts" that which is the key to our knowledge of him in all else. If we see love in our homes it is because we have love in our hearts. When the light of love goes out in our hearts it automatically goes out in our homes. Even so, if we find God without, it is because we have found him first within.

For example, we say that we see God in nature. The poet sings:

> The touch of an eternal presence thrills
> The fringes of the sunsets and the hills.[34]

But does anyone ever see God in nature who has not first found him in his own soul? We have all read books on nature written by men who were learned in her lore; many such books give no indication of having found God in nature. J. Arthur Thomson wrote *The System of Animate Nature*. He found God

[34] Richard Realf, "The Word."

in nature. John Burroughs, our great naturalist, wrote *Accepting the Universe*. He did not find God in nature. The difference between Thomson and Burroughs is that Thomson believed in God—had found him within. There is a suggestive text in the Psalms: "He healeth the broken in heart, . . . he telleth the number of the stars" (Ps. 147:3). God is known in the heart before he is seen in the stars. When therefore we say that we see God in nature, we inform nature, project on nature, our inner experience of God. As George Buttrick puts it: "God is best found in nature by those who have first found him in prayer." [35]

And is not the same true of history? Isaiah, in the temple, said: "In the year that king Uzziah died I saw the Lord" (6:1). But that does not mean that God was there in the temple for anybody to see. Two world wars in one generation are sure proof to the man of faith of God's presence in history. Yet to how many did these wars seem a complete denial of God rather than a revelation of his righteous government. How many times did we hear people say, "If there be a God why did he allow the war to break out?" Or, "If there be a God why does he not stop the war?" Such questions, besides revealing a pathetic state of Christian immaturity, show that those who have never related God to the moral forces within their own souls are ill-equipped to read his righteous judgments in the larger context of a world cataclysm. Actually, if after betraying the laws of righteousness and justice as we did, we had reaped any other harvest than tragedy, the faith of those with any moral awareness would have received a fatal blow.

[35] *Prayer*, p. 137.

Even God's revelation in Christ is missed for the same reason. Once, so John tells us, when Jesus was praying a voice was heard. And some "said that it thundered: others said, An angel spake to him" (John 12:29). So some explain the greatest personality of the ages in terms of materialism, thunder. To others he is the revealer of God. This may be partly what Richard Niebuhr has in mind when, in his learned book *The Meaning of Revelation,* he distinguishes between internal and external history, "between history as lived and history as observed by the external spectator," between "the spectator's knowledge of events" and "the participant's apprehension." [36] Those who see God in a babe lying in a manger, or in a carpenter at work at his bench, or in the prophet of Nazareth preaching by the seashore, or in a man taunted and ridiculed in Herod's hall, or hanging on a cross between two thieves, are looking with more than their physical eyes, namely, the eyes of faith. Writes Emil Brunner:

The real Christ is not visible to the historian's eye. To see the revelation of God in Christ is a gracious privilege of faith, of the believer and not of the historian; or metaphysically speaking, the organ with which Christ is apprehended is not the historian's scientific eye but the spiritual eye of the believer.[37]

Finding God within, therefore, in the inner moral sense seems to be the key to finding him without in nature or in history. "It is God who worketh in you both to will and to do of his good pleasure." (Phil. 2:13.)

[36] Pp. 81, 93.
[37] *Theology of Crisis,* p. 42.

117

It was not until after I had finished this chapter that it was brought to my attention that I had unwittingly laid the foundation for a very orthodox doctrine of the Trinity. God in nature is God the Father, God in history is God the Son, and the God within us, who helps us to detect his presence in both nature and history, is God the Holy Spirit. This coincidence itself illumines a profound Christian truth, namely, that the doctrine of the Trinity, like the deepest insights of our faith, was not invented nor arrived at through abstract theorizing but sprang out of the realities and experiences of life itself. This is why, though our way of phrasing our insights may change, their essential truth abides.

IV

THE SERMON AND THE TRUTH

LET us now consider truth specifically as it relates itself to the task of the minister. Today we speak of the sermon, a medium of expressing the truth; tomorrow of the preacher, the man who voices the truth; and finally of Christ, the embodiment of the truth, the heart of our message. To put the subjects in reverse order, we shall consider, in the next three chapters, the message, the messenger, and the manner of delivering the message—the sermon.

What the Master said of the poor, we preachers might say of our sermons—they are always with us. Never mind what the week may bring, as sure as Sunday comes the sermon. And with what disconcerting regularity do they come! We no sooner get through one than we start to get ready for another. Nor for many of us preachers do Sundays end when the day is done—they have a way of reaching over into Monday and, if the rumor is true, discoloring it! We should not, however, indulge too many disquieting reflections regarding our efforts. If we feel we have done poorly, let us console ourselves with the thought that next Sunday brings another chance. Moreover, I wonder whether a preacher is qualified to hold a post mortem on his own efforts. Our efforts cannot be quite as bad as we sometimes think they are. Nor, I am sure, are they always as good as we are at times prone to imagine!

I shall discuss the sermon under two main, though unequal, divisions. First, we shall consider the minister's workshop, where the sermon is prepared, and secondly, the literary and spiritual goals toward which the sermon should move. First, then, a word about the craftsmanship of preaching. This is not to be belittled, even though what I shall say about it must of necessity be quite personal.

Some years ago a book was published entitled *If I Had Only One Sermon to Prepare*.[1] It took the reader into the workshop of twenty-three of the great preachers of our time, Jewish, Roman Catholic, and Protestant. After reading this book I was tempted to conclude that there is no right nor wrong way of sermon preparation, since the book disclosed well-nigh as many different methods as there were men. I was reminded of the story of the boat crew of a relatively small college in Michigan who, back in the seventies, would almost invariably win their races against much larger colleges. Someone asked the old coach what kind of stroke his boys used. Was it perhaps the Harvard stroke or the Yale stroke or maybe the Oxford stroke? No, he was sure it was not any of those. "I guess," he said, "the stroke we use is the 'git thar' stroke." That is a good one for preachers to use too. Whatever method brings you "there" most effectively is the method for you. In

[1] Ed. Joseph Fort Newton.

taking you into my workshop for a few minutes I am not suggesting that you use my stroke, but only that you adopt *some* method and not leave the matter to hit and miss—for then we are sure to miss more than we hit.

For one thing I find it essential to have definite periods set aside for sermon preparation. With me these are the forenoons. Sermons should not be prepared "on the run." Sermons take work and work takes time. In keeping my engagement with the sermon I find I need tools. There is an old Chinese proverb to the effect that the weakest ink is better than the strongest memory. And when the memory is none too good to begin with, the habit of making notations proves helpful and rewarding. I have therefore evolved a filing system. It is a very simple affair of three-by-five cards on which I put subjects, illustrations, texts and quotations as they occur in my reading, observation, or experience.

Subjects come from the most unlikely places. Voltaire concludes *Candide* with a great flourish in which he advises that we should all make the best of life by going out and cultivating our gardens. As I read that sentence I looked out of the train window at the snow-covered fields that bordered the tracks, and found myself saying: "All well and good, Voltaire, but what does one do in winter?" No life ever escapes winter. It comes to all of us somehow, sometime. We need a faith for winter weather, when the very curtailment of activity forces us to reflect upon the deeper issues and meaning of our days. Of course the reverse of this truth also provides a timely subject, as Paul suggested long ago. He said that he knew not only "how to be abased" but "how to abound" (Phil. 4:12). The latter often proves to be the more difficult. Many people who stand up with courage to adversity deteriorate in prosperity. More people perchance go to pieces in the luxurious growth of summer than in the severe climate that winter brings. We need faith, then, not only for the bleak and barren days but equally for summer weather, when the sun shines, the temperature is relaxing, and the fields are lush with growing grain. Well, you see how a chance remark even by Voltaire can get you started on a subject for a sermon.

On these cards too I jot not only subjects and illustrations but texts. Every sermon that comes to my desk, whatever its source, is indexed under its text. In preparing a sermon I almost invariably read what others may have written on that particular text—assuming there is material available—despite the fact that by and large I receive so little help from this practice. This is not surprising, for a sermon is a personal piece of work, since preaching is "truth through personality." A sermon, therefore, to be effective must bear the marks of the preacher's own thought, life, and experience. If not, it will be neither true nor personal, and so no sermon at all.

In addition to subjects and texts I have found it most helpful to file away quotations. This habit is not without its dangers since one will be tempted to quote too much, a temptation to which one easily yields when he finds others saying more beautifully and effectively than he what ought to be said. Even, however, if one does not use a quotation on any given subject, just reading it over often stimulates one's own thinking and opens up new avenues of thought. I shall never use but a small part of the quotations which throughout the years I have kept on all sorts of subjects, yet I do not regret the effort spent on them. This very book is a case in point. For some fifteen years or more I have been filing away material and references on the subject of truth—just why I cannot tell. But I like to think there may have been something providential about my forethought in this matter, though I would not hold Providence responsible for the book!

I should strongly advise that we tuck away in our minds, as early in the week as possible, the text of next Sunday's sermon. It is no secret that our subconscious mind does a lot for us of which we are unaware. I like to get the text of next Sunday's sermon in my mind by Monday night. If by Tuesday noon I do not know what I am going to preach about next Sunday, I am worried. If Wednesday noon finds me still at sea, I get desperate and I am likely, in the words of one of my beloved teachers, G. A. Johnston Ross, to "mistake desperation for inspiration." Then it is that one turns more avidly than usual to *Preaching Values in the Old Testament in the Modern Translations* or *Preaching Values in the New Translations of the New Testament,* books which, like their gracious and stimulating author Halford E. Luccock, are an ever-present help in trouble.

By Monday night, then, the text or subject is in mind. Tuesday I work at something else—there is always enough of those "somethings." Wednesday forenoon I read on the particular text or subject and maybe even make a sketchy outline. Thursday and Friday and up to the middle of Saturday forenoon I write the sermon. Normally the sermon is finished by the middle of the forenoon on Saturday.

After the sermon is on paper it has to get into my system and become a part of me—I have to assimilate it. If your sermon is a part of you it will not make too much difference whether you preach without notes, from notes, or even read it. Charles Parkhurst, one of the great preachers of our generation, read his sermons and advised others to do so. Few preachers of his day, I understand, touched more deeply the life of New York city. The only time a manuscript gets between a preacher and his listeners is when the sermon on the manuscript has not become a part of the preacher. If the truth in the sermon possesses you—if you believe it, feel it, and want to share it—then your manuscript will not be an obstacle, and you will get through it to the people. If the truth does not glow in your own soul, speaking extemporaneously will be no guarantee that other hearts will be enkindled. The truth that glows in your own mind and heart will enkindle others, manuscript or no manuscript.

In writing a sermon I always try to visualize the congregation, their problems and needs. No preacher should become so interested in his subject as to forget his objects. Someone once asked a layman how he liked his new minister. "Our new minister, sir," came the reply, "can answer more questions that nobody is asking than any minister we ever had." Now it is surely a part of the minister's job to raise questions which his congregation, for one reason or another, is not asking. Good for the minister who at times disturbs his congregation by increasing their awareness of the truth. Ignorance, indifference, smugness, and self-satisfaction are formidable enemies of Christian truth against which the minister must wage war. There are times, then, when the minister ought to raise questions which do not occur to his congregation. But generally speaking, the preacher, as he prepares his sermon, should keep in mind the people whose needs he is trying to meet. One argument for preaching from an outline or extemporaneously is that this gives the preacher a freedom the fully written manuscript does not afford. For in the very act of speaking extemporaneously the congregation suggests ideas, stimulates and evokes thoughts which do not come in the detachment of study. Not so if through the use of imagination we write our sermon with our congregation in mind.

This matter of keeping the congregation in mind while preparing a sermon has yet another value. Here is a young preacher who, let us say, has a small rural parish—lucky lad! It may be, however, that the intellectual or cultural level of the congregation is not high enough to challenge or inspire his best effort. There surely is a fine chance for a young preacher to go to seed. "Like people, like priest," said Hosea. (4.9.) It is very easy for the minister in such a situation to move down to the intellectual or cultural level of his parishioners, whose requirements, as he supposes, may be met without much effort. I believe that such an assumption is false. I have found audiences of that type often more critical and exacting than more cultured ones—and more appreciative too when they realize that their minister is not talking down to them or bringing them scraps or titbits but the best effort of his mind and heart. If, however, some minister should feel that his congregation does not evoke his best effort, let him do what others have done in similar circumstances—let him, as he prepares and preaches his sermon,

125

imagine that right there in the congregation, perhaps in the front seat next Sunday morning, will be his professor of homiletics, or someone whom he greatly admires and respects. If the audience does not challenge you, create an audience that will. Those to whom you do speak deserve the finest fruitage of your mind and heart.

There is something to be said for keeping our sermons. It is interesting to see how, in the course of a few years, our approach to a text may have changed. Sometimes all that remains of a five-year-old sermon is the text. Moreover, if the stock of ministerial humility should be running low, one sure way of increasing it is to go back to the files and read over some of these "masterpieces" of other days. It is a merciful Providence that on a Sunday morning makes a minister feel that he has so much when he often really has so little. This kindly Providence seems to work not only on the minister but also on his hearers.

So much, then, for this all too informal treatment of this portion of our subject. Let us now turn to the second division of our thought, which deals not with the techniques of sermon preparation but with the goals, both literary and spiritual, which the preacher should envision as he enters his workshop.

In discussing this aspect of the matter I shall take an illustration from what is perhaps the greatest novel ever written by an American. I refer to *Moby Dick* by Herman Melville. His biographer Lewis Mumford says that Melville shares with Walt Whitman the distinction of being the greatest imaginative writer the United States has produced, and that "in depth of . . . religious insight there is scarcely any one in the nineteenth century, with the exception of Dostoyevsky, who can be placed

THE SERMON AND THE TRUTH

beside him." [2] Melville was a man of superb spiritual imagination, strength, and energy.

He lives for us not because he painted South Sea rainbows, or rectified abuses in authority in the United States Navy: he lives because he grappled with certain great dilemmas in man's spiritual life, and in seeking to answer them, sounded bottom.[3]

Melville's spiritual insight appears in that, through this gripping saga of the sea, he wrestles with the age-old problem of evil, what Paul called "the mystery of iniquity" (2 Thess. 2:7). The white whale symbolizes "the brute energies of existence—blind, fatal, overpowering." Captain Ahab, on the other hand, symbolizes "the spirit of man, small and feeble, . . . but purposive, that pits its puniness against this might, and its purpose against the blank senselessness of power." [4] But Melville's spiritual, or more specifically, homiletical insight is seen best in two short chapters in which he deals with a preacher, his pulpit, and his sermon. I have come to regard these chapters as one of the finest examples of good homiletics with which I am acquainted. Whenever anyone wants to know how to preach, to discover the marks of effective sermonizing, to understand the truths in the light of which the sermon should be prepared and preached, he can hardly do better than to sit at Melville's feet and study these passages. That is what we shall do now. First, we shall discuss what, broadly speaking, we may call the literary marks of an effective sermon, and then the spiritual marks. The

[2] *Herman Melville,* p. 4.
[3] *Ibid.*
[4] *Ibid.,* p. 184.

literary marks we shall see as we examine Father Mapple's sermon, the spiritual marks as we study the symbolism of his pulpit. First, then, the literary marks.

For one thing, Father Mapple's sermon was biblical. It was based on the book of Jonah. In the long last the most significant preaching is Bible-centered. For if it is intelligently Bible-centered it cannot avoid being life-centered, since the Bible is life in its profoundest and most meaningful orientation—its orientation Godward. Moreover, the Bible is the great textbook of the Christian religion. How can we preach or teach the Christian religion if we ignore it? Our congregations do not lack people who can inform them as well, if not better, than we about current events, but there is a great body of truth in the Bible concerning which our hearers are woefully ignorant. If the pulpit does not inform them, who will? "How shall they hear without a preacher?" (Rom. 10:14.) Preach the Bible. Never be ashamed or apologetic to do so. To preach the Bible is to ground your sermon in what is historically valid and objectively real. Our religion rests upon a body of knowledge just as objective as any other body of knowledge. It is just as impossible for a man to teach people geometry without Euclid, physics without Newton, as to teach the Christian religion without the Bible. For, as I have said, the Bible is a singularly significant portrayal of human life and experience in its profoundest relationship— its relationship with God. That is why the Bible is both relevant and imperishable: the quest for God is timeless. It is the preacher's task to make the timeless timely.

Not only so, but the preacher himself needs the Bible, needs some authority which transcends his own ingenuity. There is great reassurance and power that comes to the preacher who feels that he stands in the historic stream of a great tradition. This is his experience as he preaches from the book that bridges the centuries. To borrow a suggestive figure from Ralph Sockman:

Some preachers are like matches in that they carry all their brilliance in their own heads, and their sermons are but little unrelated flashes of cleverness caused by contact with whatever contingency has most recently rubbed against them. In contrast, the great historic doctrines of faith, like the filament of the electric light, serve as the medium of incandescence. When charged with personal feeling they become aglow with a steady light which brings the radiance of the eternal to the reading of the timely.[5]

I have a friend who never preaches from the Bible. Rather, he bases his sermons on the most recent happenings in the fields of economics, politics, religion, or the most recent ideas in sociology, psychology, or what not. I once asked him why he so completely ignored the Bible in his preaching. He replied in effect that the Bible was "old stuff," the faint echo of an age that is dead and gone. His people faced modern problems. It was his duty therefore to keep them "up-to-date"—up-to-date, this current itch that so often results in making one out-of-date. My friend's attitude is comparable to that of a man who would depend for his water supply on the latest shower of rain instead of drawing upon a reservoir or some perennial spring. I have threatened to send him a Bible for a Christmas present. For any minister who ignores the Bible on the assumption that it

[5] *Highways of God*, p. 89.

is old stuff either does not know what is in it, or else how to preach what is there.

Not only was Father Mapple's sermon biblical but it was relevant, timely, and timeliness is an unfailing mark of truth. Truth is never irrelevant. This preacher, Father Mapple, was talking to real people about real issues. His audience was a group of seafaring folk, whalers. It is perhaps more than a coincidence that his text was "The Lord had prepared a great fish to swallow up Jonah" (Jonah 1:17). We cannot always find texts that fit situations as well, nor do we need to. We do not need to be quite as literal as the famous divine who, in preaching to the girls at Wellesley College, is reported to have chosen for his text: "Follow me, and I will make you fishers of men" (Matt. 4:19). Yet our preaching must be relevant. Father Mapple's was. He was talking about Jonah, a man who lived a long time ago, yet he does not speak of Jonah as though he were a mummy, a relic of some dead age. Jonah is alive. He sits right there in the pew beside those whalers.

Of course the Bible can be preached as though it were lifeless and dull, but that is not the fault of the Bible but of the preacher. You perhaps recall the experience of George A. Gordon, of Old South Church, Boston. He and his brother went to church one morning. The sermon was on Paul. When they came out he asked his brother what he thought of the sermon, to which his brother replied; "It was a good sermon for Paul, and I am sorry he was not there to hear it." [6]

But we are not being fair to Paul, this vital, vigorous, and

[6] George A. Gordon, *My Education and Religion*, p. 118.

engaging man, when we preach him that way. It is quite possible that every word the preacher said about Paul was true, but effective preaching must do more than say what is true. It must put the truth in such a way that it hits, sticks, arrests the attention, convinces. Whenever anybody says to a preacher after a sermon, "That was meant for me this morning," or, "How did you know that I needed that sermon?" then he may be sure he is getting somewhere. He never needs to apologize when he preaches the Bible like that, nor yield to the illusion that it is out-of-date. It is as modern as the latest sin, as timely as yesterday's tragedy, as up-to-date as the most recent heartache, as perennial as man's quest for God. Like some gigantic anvil it has worn out the numberless little hammers of those who have sought to belittle its deathless insights, or to ignore and discredit its unique and indispensable place in man's spiritual development.

Let us look again at Father Mapple's sermon. Not only was it biblical and relevant; it was also direct. Note how it begins: "Shipmates, this book containing only four chapters—four yarns—is one of the smallest strands in the mighty cable of the Scriptures. Yet what depths of the soul does Jonah's deep sea-line sound!" [7] And he is off. Perhaps we preachers need not get going quite so suddenly, but I am sure that in preaching we often take too long to get started. When I sit down to write a sermon I am usually plagued by the fear that I shall not have enough to say. The result is that not infrequently after I get into the sermon, and eventually finish it, I have to go back and throw

[7] *Moby Dick*, p. 54.

the first three or four pages into the wastebasket, that good friend of every congregation. Incidentally, I never miss them! Henry Ward Beecher used to say that a text is like a gate into an open field, and that the preacher should waste no time swinging on the gate. Too often preaching is like the speech of the proverbial Irishman who started his address by saying: "My friends, before I begin to speak I want to say . . ." We often say too much before we begin to preach! Some words of Ian Maclaren come to mind:

Very likely an introduction must be written, or else the minister could not get further; but it ought then to be burned as having served its purpose. It is really getting up steam, and there is no use in inviting passengers on board till the vessel is ready to start.[8]

This is an overstatement, no doubt, but there is truth in it.

Indeed I think the difficulty of sermon preparation is not so much in having enough to say as in knowing what to leave out. As Goethe has said: "The artist is known by selection." Said Michelangelo:

The more the marble wastes,
The more the statue grows.

"If I knew how to omit," wrote Stevenson, "I should ask no other knowledge." Said Thoreau: "My stories are not long, but it took me a long time to make them short." You have probably heard of the man who was invited to make an address and

[8] William L. Stidger, *Preaching out of the Overflow*, pp. 94-95.

was asked how much time he would need to prepare. "That depends upon how long you want me to speak," he replied. "If for ten minutes, you had better give me a week's notice; if for an hour, three days will be enough; but should you want me to speak indefinitely I could begin now."

There is another characteristic of Father Mapple's sermon, as everyone who reads it will agree. Not only is it biblical, relevant, and direct but it is vivid, pictorial. "A picture is worth a thousand words," said Confucius. Notice again how the sermon begins: "Shipmates, this book, containing only four chapters—four yarns—is one of the smallest strands in the mighty cable of the Scriptures. Yet what depths of the soul does Jonah's deep sea-line sound!" Now of course Father Mapple could have said: "Shipmates, this book contains only four chapters. It is one of the smallest books of the Bible. And yet it teaches us some big lessons." That would have been just as true, but it would not have been as effective because not as vivid. As it is, one not only hears the truth Father Mapple voices; one *sees* it. You can just see those four small strands, and the mighty cable of Scripture, and the deep sea-line. Or take this. In speaking of Jonah, the fugitive, he says: "How plainly he's a fugitive! No baggage, not a hat-box, valise, or carpet-bag—no friends accompany him to the wharf with their adieux." Or this: "In this world, shipmates, Sin that pays its way can travel freely, and without a passport; whereas Virtue, if a pauper, is stopped at all frontiers." [9] Of course that is no more true than to say: "In this world, shipmates, people with

[9] *Moby Dick,* pp. 55-56.

money can get anything they want, and virtuous people without it cannot." But in the first instance you can see Sin, the passenger, traveling without a passport, and Virtue, the pauper, stopped at the frontiers. Or consider this striking picture. Jonah, the fugitive, is lying in his bunk. The ship is about to sail. His conscience is troubling him, since he knows he is dodging his duty. The ship begins to roll. He notes that the lantern hanging from the roof of the cabin maintains its perpendicular position despite the rolling of the ship, and cries: "Oh! so my conscience hangs in me! straight upward, so it burns; but the chambers of my soul are all in crookedness!" [10]

Now that is great preaching. Nobody is going to sleep on our hands if we can preach like that! Of course, you and I are not Herman Melville. He had literary gifts we do not possess. But we certainly can do better than we are doing. Dean Inge was probably right when he said that most sermons are worse than is necessary. It is not that what we say may not be true, but that the way we say it is often so terribly obvious. Somehow we must learn to take the obvious truths and put them in a fresh, surprising way. We must try to be vivid. We may say, "Jealousy destroys friendship." But suppose we say, "Jealousy, like rust, weakens the links that bind the hearts of friends." The congregation not only hear that—they see it.

One Sunday morning four pages of my sermon positively refused to attend church, so when I looked down expecting to find Page 8, I was confronted with Page 12. The situation might have been embarrassing but for the fact that I recalled

[10] *Ibid.*, p. 57.

that on those missing pages was an illustration I had borrowed from Harry Emerson Fosdick, who, incidentally, is a past master in this art of being vivid. The pages contained his illustration of the telescope. The telescope is to be looked through, not at. It should reveal, not hide the stars. So theology, like a telescope, should reveal, not veil, the eternal verities. Well, the moment I remembered that illustration everything else came to mind and I was able to assert my independence of those renegade pages. Surely this quality of vividness was one of the secrets of Jesus' effectiveness. He was never abstruse, involved, or vague but always vivid. To him the kingdom of heaven was always "like" something— "without a parable spake he not unto them" (Matt. 13:34).

Readers of Father Mapple's sermon will discover this other feature: Father Mapple stopped when he was through. It is quite evident that he was going somewhere, and when he reached his destination he stopped. I have found from my own experience that a sermon is likely either to get better as it goes along—or worse. If we are not careful our sermons may peter out. Quite often this is due not only to the fact that the minister does not know just where he is going, but to the further fact that he refuses to stop when he gets there. Lyman Abbott used to say that it was not long sermons to which people objected, but elongated sermons. There is hardly anything more deadly than an elongated sermon. Old Sam Weller of Pickwick fame has an insight it might do ministers well to remember. Sam has read his letter to his father Tony. It ends abruptly.

"That's rather a sudden pull up, ain't it, Sammy?" inquired Mr. Weller.

"Not a bit on it," said Sam. "She'll wish there was more, and that's the great art of letter writin'."

And of preaching, too. When we launch out upon our discourse we ought to have a certain port in mind. When we reach port let us find the nearest and most available pier, pull our ship alongside, stop the engines, tie her up, drop the gangplank, and let the passengers off. Let us not steam into port, head for a certain pier, and then, just as the passengers think they are about to land, back away from it, try another and then another, and sometimes still another! Perhaps the passengers have had a pleasant and profitable voyage, and this uncertainty and indecision of mussing around in the harbor looking for a place to dock might cause them to forget how pleasant the voyage has been and quite ruin the whole trip.

Here, then, are at least five of what we have called the literary marks of an effective sermon. The sermon should be biblical, relevant, direct, vivid, and have good terminal facilities.

But now let us consider the other and more important aspect of our thought. I refer to what I have called the spiritual marks of an effective sermon. To catch these deeper notes of preaching let us turn from Father Mapple's sermon to his pulpit. It is here that Melville really shows profound spiritual insight.

Father Mapple climbs up into his pulpit by a rope ladder, the kind that a pilot uses in boarding a vessel. Safely in, he leans over and draws up the ladder, which he deposits on the inside. Now how shall we interpret this symbol of physical isolation from his congregation on the part of the preacher?

What does it mean? Let us say first what it does not mean. Surely Melville did not mean to suggest that the pulpit be remote, that the minister be separated from his people, so far removed from the workaday world in which they live and move and have their being as to be incapable of even understanding their needs, let alone trying to meet them. To put any such interpretation upon this suggestion of separateness would be grossly to misinterpret it. The minister's prayer should be that of King Solomon. You will recall that when he succeeded David to the throne of Israel, God appeared to him in a dream and said: "Ask what I shall give thee." And Solomon wisely prayed: "Give . . . thy servant an understanding heart" (I Kings 3:5, 9). An understanding heart is the prerequisite of every minister. Father Mapple had that. He was preaching to a group of whalers. He himself had been a harpooner. He carried on his old weather-beaten face the marks of a sympathetic understanding of the needs and problems of those to whom he ministered. He was no armchair preacher. Recall the experience of Ezekiel, a prophet of the exile. He tells us how once he started out "in bitterness, in the heat of my spirit" (3:14), to preach a sermon to the captives. But he never preached that sermon and it is just as well that he did not. What changed him? Here are his words: "Then I came to them of the captivity at Telabib, that dwelt by the river of Chebar, and I sat where they sat, and remained there astonished among them seven days" (3:15). Every minister must vicariously try to sit where his people sit. He is most effective in the pulpit when he shares the life of the pew.

This does not mean that denunciation has no place in preaching. The truth sometimes demands it. There is such a thing as righteous indignation. There are times, no doubt, when a minister should pull out "the diapason notes of stern denunciation." The prophets did just that. One of their symbols for God was a lion. This note of severity is a normal part of any religion that seeks the truth and strives to be loyal to it. The Master himself gives proof of this, though interestingly enough he kept his denunciation not for sinners but for church people—the Pharisees. And might we not say that one reason why he denounced them was precisely because they lacked compassion, an understanding heart? They were proud, they thanked God that they were not as other men; in so far as they did this they were hypocritical. It is revealing, therefore, that the only folk with whom Jesus found it hard to be compassionate were those whose sin was a lack of compassion.

Denunciation, then, no doubt has its place. But let us never forget that we are ministers of a compassionate God, a God of love, who "is kind unto the unthankful and to the evil" (Luke 6:35). To denounce sin yet love the sinner is the Christian attitude. "There but for the grace of God go I," is the sobering truth about most of us, if not all. "Not of works, lest any man should boast." (Eph. 2:9.) Joseph Fort Newton writes truly when he says:

The preacher must know his age, love it, live in it. . . . Unless the man in the pulpit has felt the deep hurt and heartache of humanity—its bitter, blinding tragedy—unless he knows the rough places, the dangerous turns, the dismal stretches of the old, winding road, and something of what the pilgrims carry in their packs, he cannot minister to our need, much less lead us far along the way whither we seek to go.[11]

If this suggestion of withdrawal or isolation which Melville gives us by his use of the rope ladder does not mean aloofness, indifference, or a lack of understanding, what does it mean? I take it to mean that the pulpit should be free. There should be no strings attached to it. The sermon should be prepared and preached in the light of truth undimmed by fear or favor. Such is our goal, however difficult of attainment. The pulpit is separated from the church in the sense that it should not allow its message to be toned down, crippled, or sugar-coated by ulterior considerations. Not indeed that a minister is so silly as to think that he is always right in what he says, nor so bigoted as to expect his congregation to agree with all he says. His duty, however, is to "draw the Thing as he sees It for the God of Things as They Are!"[12]

This, then, is one of the spiritual marks of an effective sermon—freedom of utterance, yet a freedom based on, and tempered by, a sympathetic understanding and appreciation of the road the pilgrims travel and of what they carry in their packs. Paul said it well when he wrote to the Ephesians about "speaking the truth in love" (4:15).

Consider another insight. Directly above Father Mapple's pulpit there was painted "a little isle of sunlight, from which beamed forth an angel's face,"[13] suggesting, as you see, a

[11] *The New Preaching*, pp. 38, 40.
[12] Rudyard Kipling, "L' Envoi."
[13] *Moby Dick*, p. 52.

source of illumination that transcends the preacher, is greater than he, the divine truth, in the light of which he stands. I take this to mean that another spiritual mark of preaching is its ability to communicate to the church the sense of otherness, to convey an awareness of the eternal realities to which the preacher himself is subservient.

The minister should remember the light above him with reference to his own life. He is the leader of his church, always in the eyes of his congregation. Sometimes, in spite of all he can do, he may find some people thinking more about him than they do about God. This is particularly true in Protestantism, and perhaps especially American Protestantism. The American mind is in some ways immature. In politics we find it difficult to discuss issues objectively on their merits apart from personalities. And of course the same is equally true, if not more so, of religion. Too often does it happen that the preacher himself looms larger in the eyes of his congregation than what he preaches. The earthen vessel obscures the treasure. This is unfortunate. It may well have been to point out this danger, and so to prevent it, that Melville placed the divine light above the pulpit, transcending the preacher.

Every conscientious minister realizes that in his most effective moments he is not like a stained-glass window—something to be looked at—but like a clear-glass window, something to be looked through. He is at his best when he does not focus the light but transmits it, when, to borrow a figure, he is not like a magnetic pole drawing others to himself but a magnetic needle pointing beyond himself. To reveal realities that are greater than himself, to lead men into the presence of One whose

140

presence humbles and exalts: that is the task of the minister. It is not an easy task. We are all human. The highest fact we know is personality, and since preaching is "truth through personality" it would be impossible completely to isolate the truth from the particular personality through whom it finds expression, even if it were desirable to do so, which of course it is not. It is the *exaggerated* emphasis we must avoid and combat like that, for example, of the Corinthian Christians.

No sooner had Paul founded the church at Corinth than the people began their party cries. "One saith, I am of Paul; and another, I am of Apollos." (I Cor. 3:4.) You see, they were trying to make of Paul and Apollos stained-glass windows. So strong was the party spirit among these Corinthian Christians that Paul and Apollos, instead of being the human means through whom men were led to God, became ends in themselves and the rival objects of the church's loyalty. Such a situation was a complete denial of the truth of the gospel as Paul understood it. And so he would not tolerate their attitude. "Who then is Paul, and who is Apollos," he asked, "but ministers by whom ye believed, even as the Lord gave to every man? I have planted, Apollos watered; but God gave the increase." (I Cor. 3:5-6.) Indeed the enthusiastic folk of Lystra even began to regard Paul and Barnabas as though they were gods, and to offer sacrifices to them. The astonished Paul exclaimed: "Sirs, why do ye these things? We also are men of like passions with you, and bring you good tidings, that ye should turn from these vain things unto a living God" (Acts 14:15 A.S.V.).

Even the Master himself faced the problem. He would not allow people to make admiration of his personality an end in itself. "Why call ye me, Lord, Lord, and do not the things which I say?" (Luke 6:46.) It is as if he said: "Do not merely give me your adoration, give the truths I proclaim your loyalty." One sentimental would-be disciple cried out, "Lord, I will follow thee whithersoever thou goest" (Luke 9:57), but Jesus discouraged him, because he saw that a sentimental attachment to his person was not of itself enough save as it served to awaken loyalty to the great truths from which his personality is inseparable. Even in the hour of his death, when women were weeping for him, he could say: "Daughters of Jerusalem, weep not for me, but weep for yourselves, and for your children" (Luke 23:28)—as if to say: "What Jerusalem is doing to me today is not the issue. What Jerusalem is doing to the eternal truth I have been proclaiming, that is the issue." If even our Master could feel this way, what can ordinary people like you and me say? Surely "the servant is not greater than his lord." (John 15:20.)

Of course we want to be friends with our people. We are happy when we win their loyalty and good will. We do well to accept their affection with humble gratitude and to pray that God may make us worthy of it. But we should never forget that preaching aims to build up enduring loyalties for the abiding truths of our religion, which are from everlasting to everlasting. It was not first of all loyalty to any man, it was loyalty to Christ and to the truth God had revealed in him that kept the early church through its darkest and most difficult days. The Protestant church must be built on deeper and more enduring foundations than the precarious and uncertain fortunes of ministers.

The light above the pulpit, however, has another meaning. Not only has it a bearing on the minister himself, but also on his message. Sometimes I meet a man who says: "Oh, yes, you are at the First Baptist Church. Some Sunday I am coming up to hear what you have to say." That always sends a chill down my spine and leaves me with a sense of bankruptcy. Now, let us hope that the minister has something to say. If he has not, then he ought not to be preaching. But in preaching at its best a minister is doing something more than displaying his wares. The pulpit differs from an ordinary rostrum. It suggests something beyond the resources of the man who occupies it. For the preacher is a messenger. He has a message to deliver. And the message is not his own; he speaks for God. He attempts something more significant than just the expression of his opinions, ideas, or views about this or that. He is doing more than advertising his learning or his culture, though every minister needs both and cannot possibly have too much of either. There is a light above the pulpit, a transcendent source of illumination. This is what makes the pulpit more than a rostrum. Bernard Manning voiced a rich truth when he said: "The pulpit is no more the minister's than the communion table is his." [14]

Is not this the quality that distinguishes the Christian preacher from all the other preachers of our day? "Have you ever heard me preach?" Coleridge asked Charles Lamb one day; to which Lamb replied, "I never heard you do anything else." [15] The one thing the world does not lack today is

[14] James S. Stewart, *Heralds of God*, p. 74.
[15] *Ibid.*, p. 37.

143

preachers, all sorts and conditions of them, expounding all kinds of gospels. But the characteristic mark that differentiates the sermon of the Christian minister from all these other "sermons" is that the Christian minister views the facts of contemporary life *sub specie aeternitatis,* under the light of the eternal. The sermon aims to make known God's mind, purpose, and will—God's truth—amid all the confusion of tongues. That minister is most blessed who sends people from his church with the feeling that they have caught the echo of a tone transcending his own.

This means that the sermon itself is an integral part of worship. One occasionally sees a church service advertised as "worship and sermon." A false idea underlies that. In reality the sermon itself aims to be worshipful. The congregation should not be made to feel, when the time for the sermon comes, that they have finished with worship—sometimes disgracefully referred to as "the preliminaries"—and have come to the *pièce de résistance,* the sermon. There are no "preliminaries" in a service of worship. The minister, when he rises to preach, should feel that he is proceeding in the same spirit in which he prayed or read the Scripture. His sermon should continue in the atmosphere of worship and carry it on to greater heights. Worship should find expression in the preached word as in the Scripture, liturgy, music, or the prayers.

E. Stanley Jones, in one of his books, tells of an artist standing one day in a small mission station in India. As she stood there she was enraptured by the riot of beauty on the monsoon clouds. She exclaimed: "What a wonderful sunset, especially

144

for such a little place!"[16] The pulpit may very well seem at times to be occupying only "a little place" in the teeming life of the world. But there is a vast, eternal truth in the light of which the pulpit stands. This is the quality that gives uniqueness to the minister's message. It was this truth that Melville sought to teach as he placed above the pulpit at some focal point a ray of sunlight transcending the preacher, from which could be seen the face of the Divine. "We preach not ourselves, but Christ Jesus the Lord." (II Cor. 4:5.) That is an effective sermon which makes people aware not only of the light of our learning or of our ideas, but of the Eternal God, the light of truth, the truth that illumines our spirits and inspires our efforts.

There is a third symbolic suggestion which Father Mapple's pulpit presents. Melville writes:

Nor was the pulpit itself without a trace of the same sea-taste that had achieved the ladder and the picture. Its panelled front was in the likeness of a ship's bluff bows, and the Holy Bible rested on a projecting piece of scroll work, fashioned after a ship's fiddle-headed beak.[17]

In other words, the front of Father Mapple's pulpit was shaped like the bow of a ship. It seemed to be heading out, looking forward, going somewhere. This suggests movement, direction, adventure. The pulpit should be out in front, the first part of the church that comes in contact with the wind and waves, the tides and crosscurrents of life. There should be in

[16] *The Christ of Every Road*, p. 254.
[17] *Moby Dick*, p. 52.

145

the pulpit something of an adventurous, pioneering, prophetic spirit.

The story has it that once Henry Ward Beecher went for a walk accompanied by his dog. As they walked along the dog saw a woodchuck dart through a hole in the fence. He ran up and barked, a quite natural reaction for a normal dog. But Beecher said the interesting fact was that for days after, whenever in walking they reached that particular spot, the dog would go up to the empty hole through which the woodchuck had gone and excitedly bark his head off. You see, the dog did not realize that he was dealing with a dead issue. Dogs are not the only animals that make a lot of noise over dead issues.

It is unquestionably true that many ministers confront one of the most perplexing and discouraging problems of the modern church: too much time spent on dead issues, not enough in facing live ones. This is true theologically, as the so-called Fundamentalist-Modernist controversy has proved time and again. I am not saying that the issues raised by that controversy are necessarily of no consequence. But I do believe that our failure to see what is vital in those issues, to distinguish between theological phraseology and ideas which have changed and do change, and the enduring, underlying truths of the Christian faith, often makes that unfortunate controversy a travesty on the Christian religion. It is a serious matter indeed when one is unable to distinguish, religiously speaking, between the scaffolding and the "building of God, . . . not made with hands, eternal" (I Cor. 5:1). That is why in a world like ours, when the very survival of man seems to be at stake, the

146

average Fundamentalist-Modernist controversy strikes one as being hopelessly irrelevant.

Similarly we need to face the living issues ethically and socially. Here again we are so often behind the times. Take isolationism, for example. What a hullabaloo we have raised over that, and all wasted energy! For how anyone in his sane mind who earnestly desired world peace could have thought that our country had a choice between isolationism and world co-operation is beyond comprehension. Actually isolationism had been a dead issue for decades. Yet it took a second world war, vastly bloodier and more disastrous than the first, to convince us of that self-evident truth.

So now with the matter of national sovereignty. That too is a dead issue, for if world peace is our objective national sovereignty must go. Shall we have to be plunged into a third world war to learn that only in some kind of world government can mankind find security and peace, and that such a government is impossible so long as each nation insists on being a law unto itself—plaintiff and judge, as it were? The two positions are self-contradictory. One is reminded of the old Negro who, when asked how he happened to live a life of such inner calm and peace amid the turmoil and confusion of his day, replied: "I always tries to avoid de impossible and co-operate wid de inevitable." When shall we learn to co-operate with the inevitable and cease kicking against the goads? At any rate, whether the issues are really alive or only the artificially animated ghosts of dead ones, the pulpit must be where the issues are.

Only so can it be true to the faith. For faith is adventure—

147

"the substance of things hoped for, the evidence of things not seen" (Heb. 11:1). "By faith Abraham . . . went out, not knowing whither he went." (Heb. 11:8.) Faith is not dropping anchor in some sheltered harbor but launching out into the deep and setting sail to catch the beckoning breeze.

Something about the very age in which we live summons to adventure. For we are passing through what will unquestionably be regarded as one of the widely and deeply revolutionary periods of history. No aspect of our culture is escaping. It seems as though the words of the unknown author of Hebrews were being fulfilled. "I shake not the earth only, but also heaven." (Heb. 12:26.) Our gospel should be at home in such an age for it is a revolutionary gospel. In our hands it so often stands on the side of the status quo, but when it first came into the world it struck terror into the hearts of the defenders of the status quo. If its searching insights no longer burn, if we can repeat the great sentences of our faith without being thrilled, it is because, as Charles E. Jefferson said, we have forgotten that "whenever men truly grasp them, they work renaissances, reforms, and revolutions."

That is what they did in the first century. The apostles were followers of one whom they regarded as the "pioneer . . . of faith" (Heb. 12:2 Moffatt). Jesus was an adventurer in the finest meaning of that term. The proof of that is his cross, which was the direct result of his moral and ethical pioneering. "He stirreth up the people," said his enemies. (Luke 23:5.) He cannot help but disturb anyone in any age who seriously accepts his two major doctrines of the fatherhood of God and its corollary the brotherhood of man. If we Christians today

148

really believed these doctrines as Jesus believed them, they would create such a revolution in the social order as we have never seen.

The early apostles were revolutionaries, men who "turned the world upside down." This was because they took seriously the message of Jesus. They did not keep in step with their age. "Be not conformed to this world," they said. (Rom. 12:2.) Their gospel was not the gospel of accommodation to the world as they found it, but of reconciliation. "Now then we are ambassadors for Christ, as though God did beseech you by us: we pray you in Christ's stead, be ye reconciled to God." (II Cor. 5:20.) This is why they were adventurers, for to be reconciled to God is to be irreconciled to all that thwarts the will of God. We cannot be reconciled to God if at the same time we cherish evil purposes, indulge in evil practices, or tolerate evil conditions either in ourselves or in our world, which are at variance with the nature and will of God as made known in Christ. The Scripture states succinctly that law of reconciliation: "Ye that love the Lord, hate evil" (Ps. 97:10).

That was the principle the apostles followed. That is why they lived creatively, adventurously. They did not accept the world. Too often we do. We fail to realize that to adjust ourselves to one set of forces is to throw ourselves out of gear with reference to another set. A little girl playing seesaw with her brother began to cry because, said she: "I want to go up when Johnny goes up, and I want to go down when Johnny goes down." Some of us older boys and girls need constantly to be reminded of the impossibility of such moral acrobatics. The apostles did not attempt that. They were in the world but not of it. They looked "for new heavens and a new earth, wherein dwelleth righteousness" (II Pet. 3:13). They were adventurers.

Strangely enough, however, they never used the phrase "the social gospel," nor did they speak as do we about "social problems," but their gospel of reconciliation to God in Christ profoundly shook the world, changed radically the course of history. Paul, for example, did not attack slavery as such. He sent back a runaway slave, Onesimus, to his master Philemon. But with the slave went a letter, part of which reads: "I beseech thee for my son Onesimus, whom I have begotten in my bonds, . . . that thou shouldst receive him; . . . not now as a servant, but above a servant, a brother beloved, . . . both in the flesh, and in the Lord. If thou count me therefore a partner, receive him as myself" (Philem. 1:10, 15-17). Now really, just how long do you suppose Philemon could regard Onesimus as "a brother beloved" and continue to treat him as a slave? How long do you suppose you or I could regard one of another race as "a brother beloved" and still make him the object of cruel, humiliating and unjust racial discrimination, or the victim of a system, economic, social, or political, that dwarfs or destroys his personality? Maybe the apostles were not concerned about social problems as such, but they took seriously the gospel of reconciliation to God through Christ, which if practiced would revolutionize the social order.

No wonder then that the early Christians revolutionized society. They took Jesus seriously. The gospel is still potentially a revolutionary gospel, that is why it is at home in a revolutionary era. It has more chance when the waters are disturbed than when they are stagnant; when men are aroused than when they are asleep. The finest insights of our religion did not come out of untroubled periods of peace and plenty. They came out of exile, persecution, crucifixion. "Woe to them that are at ease in Zion." (Amos 6:1.) "Woe to him who seeks to pour oil upon the waters when God has brewed them into a gale!" [18] The very unrest of our age may be God's challenge to us to fashion the world nearer to Jesus' ideal of brotherhood under God's universal fatherhood. This may seem in such an age the most hopeless and impossible of tasks. In plain truth it is man's best ground for hope. To realize this hope the adventurous, pioneering spirit is essential.

How one wishes the pulpit could merit the great confidence that Herman Melville places in it! In referring to the symbol of the prow he writes:

What could be more full of meaning?—for the pulpit is ever this earth's foremost part; all the rest comes in its rear; the pulpit leads the world. From thence it is the storm of God's quick wrath is first described, and the bow must bear the earliest brunt. From thence it is the God of breezes fair or foul is first invoked for favorable winds. Yes, the world's a ship on its passage out, and not a voyage complete; and the pulpit is its prow.[19]

To the quality, therefore, of freedom, which makes one speak the truth in love, and the communicating of the sense of otherness, which reveals the truth that is higher than man, we must add the adventurous, pioneering spirit. We follow One who goes before us and whom we shall never overtake.

[18] *Moby Dick*, p. 61.
[19] *Ibid.*, p. 52.

V

THE PREACHER AND THE TRUTH

Bishop William A. Quayle once inquired: "Is preaching the art of making a sermon and delivering it?" He answered his question by saying: "Why, no, that is not preaching. Preaching is the art of making a preacher and delivering that. It is no trouble to preach, but a vast trouble to construct a preacher." [1] There is profound truth in that observation. The preacher is like an instrument. He must be in tune to be an effective medium of expression. For he is at his best when he is transmissive, when something happens through him rather than by him. "He is a chosen vessel unto me, to bear my name before the Gentiles." (Acts 9:15.) Indeed the words of saints and seers leave us in no doubt that their lives were marked by this transmissive quality. They sometimes regarded themselves as being just a "voice" speaking for One to whose righteous will and holy purpose they sought to submit their lives.

This sense of being used by God is often made clear to the minister in the very act of preaching. Henry van Dyke was once asked whether or not it was hard to preach. He replied: "No,

[1] James S. Stewart, *Heralds of God,* p. 190.

it is not hard to preach; but it is very hard to bring oneself to the mood where one is fit to preach." [2] That mood is one of conscious dependence upon God, who, if the preacher is worthy, will use him for his glory. If it is true, as John Ruskin once observed, that the duty of the clergyman is to remind people in an eloquent manner of the existence of God, then the preacher must be in tune with God if he is to fulfill that obligation. Let us then think of the words of Paul addressed to Timothy. They have a peculiar relevance for ministers. Said he: "Study to show thyself approved unto God, a workman that needeth not to be ashamed, rightly dividing the word of truth." (II Tim. 2:15.) Let that serve as the text for this chapter on the preacher and the truth.

One observation must be made at the outset about this workman: his job is too big for him. Part of its difficulty is its size. For example, the minister must read but he seldom reads widely or deeply enough. And no wonder, for any book upon any subject whatsoever that increases knowledge, stirs the imagination, or enriches life, is grist for his mill. His field is the world of literature. It is no doubt true that some few ministers read too much and do not think enough. Their sermons are undigested homilies bearing unmistakable evidence of the latest book they have read but lacking the mellowness that comes from reflection and meditation. Milton speaks of one

who reads
Incessantly, and to his reading brings not
A spirit and judgment equal or superior,

[2] William Adams Brown, *Life of Prayer in a World of Science,* p. 162.

153

. . . .
> Uncertain and unsettl'd still remains,
> Deep vers'd in books and shallow in himself.[3]

I venture, however, that should the average minister be "shallow in himself," this is not because he is "deep vers'd in books."

If the minister calls, he does not call enough. Perhaps in the midst of writing a sermon there will come to his mind the names of neglected parishioners. If he tries to comfort those that mourn, he wishes he could give to them more of his time and of himself. If he writes to his servicemen or college students, he does not write often enough. If he sends notes of appreciation to those in his church whose helpful spirit has inspired his own, there are yet others who should receive them but do not. If he comes to know some of the boys and girls in the church school so that he can call them by their first names, there are still others, the majority, whose faces he recognizes but whose names he does not know. "He calleth his own sheep by name." (John 10:3.) So it was said of the Master. In a large church the minister sometimes does not know their names, he knows only their number. It all adds up to this: our job is too big for us. I am frank to confess that often I am more disturbed by the things left undone than am I reassured by what I have tried to do. Not only so, but there are no hours off in this job. A bishop of Chester one day reproved one of his incumbents for drunkenness.

"But, my lord," protested the surprised cleric, "I was never drunk on duty!"

[3] *Paradise Regained.*

"On duty!" thundered the bishop, "pray, sir, when is a clergyman not on duty?" [4]

Well, there you have it! Yet the size of the task is nothing for the workman to be ashamed of; rather he should be thankful that God has called him to a task so challenging and engrossing that he cannot easily encompass it.

Now let us look at this workman, who needeth not to be ashamed. In his epistle to the Romans, Paul writes: "For I am not ashamed of the gospel of Christ" (Rom. 1:16). In this letter to Timothy, however, he strikes as it seems to me a deeper note. He is not saying: "I am not ashamed of the Gospel"; he is rather concerned that the gospel be not ashamed of him—"a workman that needeth not to be ashamed." I propose to discuss four characteristic marks of that workman.

The first mark is industry. The workman who needs not be ashamed will be an industrious workman. The cause of truth will not be helped by sluggards. David Christie, in his little classic *The Service of Christ*, says that there are three great temptations every minister faces:

> The temptation to recline.
> The temptation to shine.
> The temptation to whine.[5]

It is the first of these that now concerns us—the temptation to recline. The ministry is the last place on earth for a lazy man. There is no substitute in the Christian ministry for downright hard work and lots of it. The man who wants an easy

---

[4] Albert D. Belden, *George Whitefield, the Awakener*, p. 55.
[5] P. 66.

berth had better flee the ministry as though it were a plague. "I would have laziness held to be the one unpardonable sin in all our students and in all our ministers," said Alexander Whyte.[6] The minister must be industrious.

By industry I do not mean just being busy. It is possible to be terribly busy; like Martha, to be careful and troubled about so many things that there is little time for matters of first importance. There is scarcely a profession in which a man can be more busy and accomplish less than in the ministry. By industrious I mean being intelligently and purposefully occupied. "One thing I do," said Paul. (Phil. 3:13.) His words are helpful in that they reveal the need of having some major goal around which, as a powerful magnet, our efforts so often scattered and fragmentary are pulled into line.

A part of this industry will be intellectual—study. The intellectual demands on a modern minister are far greater than those his fathers faced. George Matheson once came to the defense of preachers who were called "high" and "low" by declaring there was one worse than either, namely, the preacher who was "thin." [7] The story has it that a minister once recognized as the most regular attendant at the worship service a hard-working washerwoman who Sunday after Sunday was observed in her pew. He wanted to find the reason for such fidelity and so asked: "Is it that you enjoy the beautiful music?"

"Na, it's no' that."

"Perhaps you enjoy my sermons?"

"Na, it's no' that."

[6] G. F. Barbour, *Life of Alexander Whyte,* p. 282.
[7] D. MacMillan, *Life of George Matheson,* p. 246.

"Then what brings you here every week?"

"Weel, it's like this. I work hard a' week, and it's no' often I get sic a comfortable sate wi sae little tae think aboot."

We owe it to our people to give them something to "think aboot." To stimulate the mind may be one way of restoring the soul. Bishop Winnington-Ingram, of London, on a visit to the United States some years ago, said he observed that nearly every American minister had a telephone and an automobile, but that comparatively few had a worth-while library. At any rate, we must study. It must not be true of us that our sermons are "not good enough to make men think, nor bad enough to make men sleep." [8] We must present our people with something more than what Charles Lamb called "the self-sufficiency of surpliced emptiness."

Yet I am not pleading for sermons that are coldly intellectual. George MacLeod, of Iona, Scotland, put the matter well when he said:

It is not that our clergy are too intellectual. . . . It is that we are apt to be only intellectual. As an honest old Scotch minister once protested: "The meenistry of the Kirk o' Scotland is the most ed-dicated meenistry in the worrld and it has verra nearly ruined the Kirk o' Scotland." [9]

A preacher who gives light but no warmth is only half a preacher. We worship a God of love, who "healeth the broken in heart" (Ps. 147:3). The God whom Christ revealed is one of compassion, grace, and mercy. He rejoices over a returning

[8] John M. Versteeg, *Perpetuating Pentecost*, p. 118.
[9] *Christian Century*, January 22, 1947, p. 109.

prodigal, and goes out in loving concern to find one lost sheep. Not even the fall of a sparrow escapes his infinite and tender concern. The preacher speaks for this compassionate God. A coldly intellectual preacher who deems it improper to stir people's emotions or reach their hearts will not be able adequately to transmit the truth that God has made known.

It is true that Paul warned against zeal without knowledge, yet I am sure that in no sense was he advocating knowledge without zeal. When an unbalanced, impulsive woman appeared at Wesley's meetings he refused to allow her to be banned. "How much preferable is her irregular warmth to the cold wisdom of them that despise her!" he said. We are to give reason for the faith that is in us, but our religion must not be "so very reasonable as to have nothing to do with the heart and affections." [10]

Perhaps a good example of the proper balance between the intellect and the emotions is provided by Benjamin Haydon, who was considered by such of his contemporaries as Wordsworth, Scott, and Keats as one of the bright lights of the English culture of his time. He was an artist and had as his great ambition painting the face of Christ. Something of the devoutness of his spirit is seen in his words: "The moment I touch a great canvas, I think I see my Creator smiling on all my efforts; the moment I do mean things for mere subsistence, I feel as if he had turned his back, and what's more I believe it." In 1817, as he was beginning to plan for a picture of Jesus' entry into Jerusalem, he jotted down this sentence: "I resolved

[10] James Moffatt, *Love in the New Testament*, p. 207.

to acquire the fundamental principles of perspective, of which I did not know enough. I earnestly prayed that I might conceive and execute such a picture of the head of Christ as would impress the Christian world." [11] There you have it—"I earnestly prayed." Here was a devout soul. But, "I resolved to acquire the fundamental principles of perspective." This technical requirement could be met only when to his prayer he added study.

So with us. To our religious zeal we must add knowledge. The minister will have many seemingly good and proper reasons for neglecting his periods of study, but never mind how good they seem, they are not good enough. Mary Heaton Vorse once said, "The art of writing is the art of applying the seat of the pants to the seat of the chair." [12] This aphorism, though crude, voices a truth that every minister would do well to remember. A preacher who does not have definite periods set apart for uninterrupted study is not being fair to himself, his church, nor to his Master.

Another mark of "a workman that needeth not to be ashamed" is integrity. "Preaching can survive countless honest errors; it cannot stand insincerity." So writes Dean Willard Sperry of Harvard.[13] "What one *is*," says Georgia Harkness, "affects what one *thinks*, and therefore what one declares to be the truth." [14] The ministry, as I have come to know it, differs from other professions or vocations in this at least, that

[11] James Moffatt, *Jesus Christ the Same*, p. 10.
[12] *Reader's Digest*, January, 1938, p. 80.
[13] *We Prophesy in Part*, p. 126.
[14] *The Faith by Which the Church Lives*, p. 46.

it takes all of a man. Paul tells us to present our bodies a living sacrifice. We are admonished to love the Lord our God with all our heart, our soul, our mind. That is to say, the whole man is involved. Nowhere are fractions so improper as in the ministry. The need here is for the integer—the whole number. The English word "holy" derives from the Anglo-Saxon "hale," which means whole.

This is not so true of some other callings. A man may make good clothes and yet not be a good man. Some whose artistic gifts we have admired have lived notoriously indulgent and undisciplined lives. It is conceivable even that a man may be a good doctor and not be a good man—though admittedly he would be a better doctor if he were—but not so with the physician of souls. The doctor diagnoses an ailment and writes a prescription for his patient. The minister must take his own medicine before it can effectively help another. In the Christian ministry it is peculiarly true that a "man's work can never be better than the man himself." [15] The ministry claims the whole man. The minister cannot effectively help others to win the victory over evils to which he himself surrenders. The minister is to bear witness to the truth, but the truth cannot effectively be borne in a broken vessel.

I sometimes think that the very professional aspect of ministerial work may tend to obscure the moral obligations which are as incumbent on us as on the humblest and most obscure Christian. The fact is, however, that in Protestantism professional or ecclesiastical authoritarianism can never be made a substitute for moral and spiritual integrity. In Protes-

[15] *Crozer Quarterly,* January, 1929, p. 22.

tantism it is not the clergyman per se that we respect but the man in the clergyman. I find nothing in the Bible to make me believe that God has the slightest respect for "the cloth" as such. Indeed we have every reason to think that God is not cloth conscious at all, since "the Lord seeth not as man seeth; for man looketh on the outward appearance, but the Lord looketh on the heart" (I Sam. 16:7). In fact, rightly or wrongly, a good deal more is expected of a man who happens to be a clergyman. His official position does not shield him but on the contrary exposes him to the most critical scrutiny. Blessed is the man of such integrity that he needs not be ashamed.

There is another reason besides professionalism which might prove a handicap. It is that the preacher is in constant danger of mistaking his use of the great words and ideas of the gospel for his firsthand experience of them. "Great words tempt the speaker," said G. A. Studdert-Kennedy, "that is why he needs to say his prayers." [16] Paul sensed this peril, hence his fear "lest that by any means, when I have preached to others, I myself should be a castaway." (I Cor. 9:27). The preacher spends so much time in instructing other people in the way of life that he may forget that it is only as he tries to live the life that his instruction becomes meaningful. In one's zeal to reform the world it is easy to forget that the proper place to start is with one's self.

There is an illuminating example of this truth in the book of Ezra. After many years of exile Artaxerxes had authorized the return of the captives to Jerusalem. Ezra the scribe returned with them and set himself to the task of teaching them

[16] *The Word and the Work*, p. 75.

the law of God. This is what we read: "For Ezra had prepared his heart to seek the law of the Lord, and to do it, and to teach in Israel statutes and judgments" (7:10). Moffatt translates the passage: "Ezra had set his heart upon studying the law of God, upon obeying it, and upon teaching its rules and regulations in Israel." You see, he began with himself. He studied it and sought to obey it before he began to teach it. His preparation was twofold: intellectual—studying; moral—obeying. Both the intellectual and moral aspects are necessary but the moral is more than necessary. It is indispensable.

Now of course I am not suggesting that one ever actually lives up to the gospel he preaches; yet even though we cannot live up to it, we must sincerely strive to. "Not that I have already obtained, or am already made perfect: but I press on, if so be that I may lay hold on that for which also I was laid hold on by Christ Jesus." (Phil. 3:12-13 A.S.V.) Though he did not reach the goal, Paul kept it ever in view and strove towards it. Robert Louis Stevenson has put the matter well:

No man can do as well as he teaches. For we are all like St. Paul in this, that we see better things than we are able to attain to; we cannot therefore hope to be seen doing what we teach, but we must be seen trying to do it: we shall even only teach it well, in so far as we are trying hard. The man who only talks, I pledge you my word, he will not even do the talking well.[17]

Outside the town of Winchester, England, is the quaint old priory of St. Cross. In the church is a lectern, an eagle with spreading wings, carved out of oak. As I once examined the

[17] Graham Balfour, *Life of Robert Louis Stevenson*, II, 227.

lovely carving I observed this strange fact, that while the bird was an eagle all right, with mighty wings, his beak was not the beak of an eagle but the bill of a parrot. It seemed such an undignified modification to put on this otherwise majestic bird—a squawking and chattering parrot's bill. I observed further that on the head of the eagle there was carved a heart. I pointed out these strange facts to the old verger and asked what they meant. He said that a parrot's bill had been substituted for the eagle's beak and a heart placed on the eagle's head so that when the minister goes to the lectern to read the Scripture he will remember that he is not to read it like a parrot but from the heart.

Well, that holds good not only for reading the Scripture but for all aspects of the minister's work. This task demands not only our minds but our hearts; not only our lips but our lives—integrity, the whole man, all there is of him. There is an old proverb: "Not the cry but the flight of the wild duck leads the flock to fly and follow." Or, in the soberer language of Thomas Carlyle: "To teach religion, the first thing needful, and the last, and indeed the only thing is to find a man who has religion." [18] For in the long last the greatest sermon a minister ever preaches is never preached, it is lived; it is not written on paper but in life: "Ye are our epistle written in our hearts, known and read of all men" (II Cor. 3:2).

A third mark of the workman who needs not be ashamed is interest, interest in people. The truth which the minister proclaims is not an impersonal or abstract truth. It is, on the contrary, truth that is meant for persons, and is therefore best

[18] Frank Cairns, *The Prophet of the Heart*, p. 180.

mediated through lives that exemplify a warm interest in people. The preacher needs to be widely alive. He must be sensitive without being touchy, sympathetic without being sentimental. He must have an understanding spirit without being indiscriminately agreeable, and be genuinely interested without being inquisitive. In short, he must love both the people and the truth. If he is human he may not be able to like everybody, but he must love those whom he may not like; that is to say, he must maintain toward them the Christian spirit of resolute good will. Some of the "saints" do not make the most agreeable of companions. As the little jingle puts it:

> To live with the saints in Heaven
> Is bliss and glory;
> To live with the saints on earth
> Is—often another story! [19]

Spurgeon used to say of some persons in his church: "They must have been sent into the world, not that I might save their souls, but that they might discipline mine." [20] Most churches do not lack these ministerial disciplinarians.

It is always good for the minister to "remember . . . Jesus Christ" (II Tim. 2:8 A.S.V.), but never more so than in his dealings with people. Said an old minister: "If I had my ministry over again, I would spend three quarters of the time I have spent in making sermons in making friends." [21] We must allow for the natural overemphasis of the epigram, yet it is

[19] *Atlantic Monthly*, October, 1928.
[20] David Christie, *The Service of Christ*, p. 87.
[21] Richard Roberts, *The Untried Door*, p. 149.

evident that here we seem to encounter a principle of Jesus. In the fine phrase of T. R. Glover: "Jesus understood the individual, and had leisure for him." [22] There are at least five words he used to express his relationship with men. He thought of them as his followers, sometimes as his disciples, then again as witnesses, once more as servants—but he also called them his friends. Followers, disciples, witnesses, servants, friends. The relationship of friends is the most significant of all, for it suggests a sharing of inner thoughts, purposes and plans—of spirit. "No longer do I call you servants; for the servant knoweth not what his lord doeth: but I have called you friends; for all things that I heard from my Father I have made known unto you." (John 15:15 A.S.V.)

A workman that needs not be ashamed will therefore keep alive his interest in folk. He will remember that the friendly contacts he makes as man with men will be among the most important and rewarding of his ministry. And, mark you, I do not mean just a general interest in mankind. It is easy to be sentimental about mankind and indifferent to man. Jesus did not say much about mankind but he had some deeply significant dealings with men. So far as we know he did not appear before the Rotary Club in Jerusalem, but he made very meaningful contacts with some men who no doubt would have belonged: Nicodemus, Zacchaeus, the rich young ruler. He did not address the Galilean Fishermen's Convention, but he said to a fisherman, "Follow me" (Matt. 4:19). He preached to the multitude. Had he done nothing more I fear we might never have heard of him. It was not the multitude who saw him after

---

[22] *Jesus in the Experience of Men*, p. 191.

his resurrection. It was not to the multitude that he said: "Lovest thou me more than these? . . . Feed my sheep" (John 21:15-16). "All authority hath been given unto me. . . . Go ye therefore, and make disciples of all the nations. . . . And lo, I am with you always, even unto the end of the world." (Matt. 28:18-20 A.S.V.) Christianity survived because of a few loyal souls who were so united to Christ that neither life nor death, nor things present nor things to come could separate them from him. This is no reflection on crowds. Every minister loves crowds, especially at eleven o'clock on Sunday morning. And they are a great inspiration indeed, if he is fortunate enough to have them. I am only saying that perhaps in the long last his most valuable and significant ministry will be measured in terms of what he might have been privileged to do for, and with, individual men and women. The crowd knows a great preacher but the individual knows a true friend who, because of his kindly interest, stood by him and shared with him his bane or blessing. So it was with the Master.

The story has it that Mrs. Humphrey Ward wrote a letter once to a member of parliament regarding a poor family in his district. The member to whom she wrote was a man who always manifested great interest in social welfare and invariably sponsored legislation which would bring it about. She was surprised therefore to have this man write her as follows: "I am so busy with plans for the race that I have no time for the individual." Mrs. Ward filed the letter away with this observation written across it: "Our Divine Lord, when last heard from, had not attained this sublime altitude." [23] "God so loved the world"—

[23] Charles T. Holman, *The Religion of a Healthy Mind*, p. 104.

that is a magnificent concept. But just suppose that were all
we knew about God, that he loved the world. "Christ . . . loved
the church." (Eph. 5:25.) That is more meaningful because
more personal. "Christ . . . loved me, and gave himself up for
me." (Gal. 2:20 A.S.V.) That rings the bell! We shall never
surrender or silence the challenging social note of our gospel,
but the power of this gospel of ours lies in its amazing claim
that the eternal God cares for individuals like you and me;
indeed, that the eternal God who loves the world cannot re-
deem it save as he does so by redeemed individuals. The God
whom Jesus revealed is not just Creator but Father, and the
essence of fatherhood is concern for each child in the family.

What I am saying is that the Christian minister must be
not only preacher reaching the group, but pastor maintaining
a personal interest in individuals. No concern for mankind in
general can be made a substitute for his interest in and care for
individuals in particular. Our business, then, is personal business. Jesus mediated truth to people not just through his words
but through himself—"There went virtue out of him" (Luke
6:19). In like manner must we share our life with people. At
the end of a successful morning's writing Tolstoy joyously
exclaimed: "I have once more left a particle of myself in the
inkstand." You and I too will at times have that joyous experience as we write in our study. But not only in the inkstand
will we leave a particle of ourselves. We will leave it in some
hospital room, where death has set his mark on the face of a
child, or on a youth in the glad morning of his days. We will
leave it in some humble home, where a grief-stricken couple
mourn the loss of their only son, or in some elegant home where

167

wealth and social prestige were powerless to stay the hand of tragedy or deepest grief. We will leave ourselves, yet not just ourselves. For the friendship the minister mediates when he stands with others in the valley of the shadow possesses a quality that is more than human. The minister tries to bring to others the consolations of God, to make them aware of the Eternal, who is their refuge and strength. So you will go to them not only as a friend of man but as a friend of God, who brings with his human friendship that touch that is more than human —a knowledge of the truth which is their strength and shield.

Here, then, are three marks of the workman who needs not be ashamed: industry, integrity, interest. There is a fourth— independence. This may seem almost to contradict what I have just said. Yet not so. For by independence I do not mean that the minister is sufficient unto himself. Indeed there is scarcely a profession or vocation that needs more the sympathetic support and co-operation of one's fellows than the ministry. Every church could say reverently to its minister what Jesus said to his disciples: "Apart from me ye can do nothing" (John 15:5 A.S.V.). The minister is a leader; but a leader must have followers, so the minister constantly needs the support of loyal hearts and willing hands. I am reminded of a cartoon I saw some years ago of the Toonerville trolley inching its way along. An irate passenger, who probably had to make a train connection, came up excitedly to the motorman and blurted: "Can't you run any faster than this?"

"Sure I can," replied the motorman, "but I have to stay with the car!"

Well, this car, the church, moves slowly. Often the minister wishes it would move faster, but he has to stay with it, unless perchance he should be one of those honored souls whom God sometimes calls to blaze a new trail, break with the organized church, even as did the Master, and pioneer the path of man's spiritual pilgrimage. Sometimes the earthen vessel has to be broken to save the treasure. When therefore I speak of the minister as being independent, I do not mean that he is self-sufficient or lacking in understanding. I mean that in the work of the ministry he will put first his loyalty to truth. In the brave words of Peter he "must obey God rather than men" (Acts 5: 29 A.S.V.). "Study to show thyself approved *unto God.*" (II Tim. 2:15.)

There is therefore a tension between the gospel and the ideas or ideals which obtain in secular society. The Kingdom of God is "not of this world," as the Master said (John 18:36). In this fact lies its redemptive power, because only that which is not of this world is able to transform the world. Christianity makes a difference in society because it is different from society. As the difference becomes progressively indistinct its effectiveness in society becomes progressively impaired. To give the people what they want is not the minister's business. He must aim to give them what they need. His task is not to please them but to serve them.

Once when the kings of Judah and Israel, Jehosaphat and Ahab, conspired to make war against Syria, they inquired of the prophets whether the expedition would be successful. The "prophets" they consulted were yes men and prophesied that all would go well. But there was one prophet, Micaiah by name, whose opinion Ahab, the king of Israel, particularly wanted.

"I hate him," said Ahab, "for he doth not prophesy good concerning me, but evil." (I Kings 22:8.) A messenger therefore was sent to Micaiah and said to him: "Behold now, the words of the prophets declare good unto the king; . . . let thy word . . . be like the word of one of them, and speak that which is good. And Micaiah said, As the Lord liveth, what the Lord saith unto me, that will I speak." (I Kings 22:13-14.) His aim, you see, was not to please but to serve. His first loyalty was to truth as he saw it.

Dean Inge, in his caustic manner, once wrote: "The way to be successful is to give the public exactly what it wants, and about 10 per cent more of it than it expects." [24] But the preacher does not want that kind of success. When the politician gives the people what they want, it is in order to get from the people what he wants—votes. This accounts for our tragic lack of courageous political leadership. It explains the appalling obscurantism and corruption which hang like a millstone about the neck of our democratic processes. It means government by opportunism and expediency rather than by principle. It means that we are caught in a vicious circle, the blind leading the blind, and explains why politically speaking we are not only nationally but internationally so often in the ditch. The preacher cannot be party to that principle. As a witness to the truth his primary concern is not to "gratify men's appetites" but to "improve their tastes."

This is what Christianity should do for us even though in so doing it goes against the grain, gets under the skin, or rubs us the wrong way. Someone remarked to Dean Inge that few

[24] James S. Stewart, *Heralds of God*, p. 29.

170

people attend church. He is reported to have replied that there would be fewer people still if the gospel were preached in them! Maybe not, but in any event the preacher must remember that the gospel loses its power when, chameleonlike, it takes on the color of the secular age—"be not conformed to this world" (Rom. 12:2). Indeed, the aim of the preacher should be that of developing in his people a Christian mind. We should try to give them, not the Democratic nor the Republican slant on things, not the capitalistic nor labor union's outlook, not the American point of view—except in so far as these may be on the side of Christian truth as we understand it—but the Christian point of view. Should it not be our aim to try to develop in ourselves and in others a *collective Christian mind?*

The need of a Christian, as opposed to a secular, outlook was seen from Old Testament days. Consider this illuminating text in Leviticus. The children of Israel had escaped from Egypt and were about to establish themselves in Canaan. This is the command God gave them through Moses: "You must not copy the practices of Egypt, where you lived, nor the practices of Canaan, whither I am taking you; you must not rule your lives by theirs. Follow my regulations, keep my rules, and live by them; I am the Eternal your God" (Lev. 18:3-5 Moffatt). That is an amazing religious insight to come from so early a period of mankind's spiritual pilgrimage. The words may be paraphrased as follows: "You are to establish a religious civilization, therefore you must not mold it after that of the country from which you have come, nor yet must it be like that of the country to which you are going. You must be independent of both of these. You must obey my command, be loyal to the

insights I shall give you; you must develop a different mind."
"Have this mind in you, which was also in Christ Jesus." (Phil.
2:5 A.S.V.) There is an old saying, perhaps an exaggeration yet
largely true: "He who would do anything for the world must
have nothing to do with it."

The principle involved here goes back to Isaiah. Up to his
time the Hebrew nation was regarded *in toto* as the church.
There was no distinction between a religious community with
a distinctive mind-set as opposed to the nation. Whatever the
nation did was looked upon as an expression of the purpose of
God. The church and the state were one. During the exile,
however, while the majority fell to imitating the practices of
their pagan captors, Isaiah visualized a small group, a "remnant," who would not conform. "A remnant shall return, even
the remnant of Jacob, unto the mighty God." (Isa. 10:21 A.S.V.)
In a real sense this was the beginning of the church. This was
the first time in history that a religious minority, a group who
dared to think differently, was ever shaken loose from the
general mass. The remnant was an Israel within Israel, a group
who judged its environment in the light of God's transcendent
truth. The remnant came to its full historic flowering in the
church, the "ekklesia"—"a calling out," "a colony of heaven,"
as Paul named it (Phil. 3:20 Moffatt).

It is no wonder that the early church was different from its
environment. Thoreau said that if a man did not keep step with
his age perhaps it was because he heard a different drummer.
It is quite evident that the early Christians did just that—they
heard a different drummer. They would not keep step with an
age that was out of step. They were not feeble echoes of the

world's voice, but the voice of God to the world. They did not conform to the world but sought to transform it by bringing to it new and different spiritual insights. They were not dough but leaven. They were different. This explains their amazing impact upon their age.

A Church which is at home in society and voices its prevailing views can have nothing redeeming to say to it. It must make its members critics of whatever is in order that they may become creators with Christ of what should be.[25]

There has been much talk in certain quarters about producing people who are perfectly adjusted to their environment. There are, to be sure, certain factors in one's environment which, like Paul's "thorn in the flesh," are with us always. Like him we may beseech "the Lord thrice, that it might depart" (II Cor. 12:8), only to find that it cannot be removed. But there follows the promise: "My grace is sufficient for thee" (II Cor. 12:9). Through the grace of God many brave souls have been able to adjust themselves and have won magnificent victories over the most untoward circumstances.

The idea of adjustment, as popularly used, however, does not mean that. It suggests rather that a man, chameleonlike, should take on the color of his age, that his life, like the waters of a swamp, should just ooze out and accommodate itself to the particular contour of the land. This is a wholly unchristian idea. When the rear wheels of a car are stuck in the mud the car may be said to be completely adjusted to its environment. The trouble with it, however, is that it is stuck! What is needed then

[25] Henry Sloane Coffin, *Religion Yesterday and Today*, p. 173.

173

is a lever to lift the wheels to a higher frame of reference. It was just such a lever that Christianity brought into the world. Pilate, the opportunist—there was a perfectly adjusted individual for you! But the man who stood before him was not so adjusted. He would not give the people what they wanted, indulge their prejudices and condone their sins. Rather he sought to lift them to a higher level as he pioneered a righteousness which exceeded the inadequate traditional standards in which their lives had been set. His cross stands in history as a symbol of his amazing loyalty to the truth, and the assurance of his continuing power in transforming the world by renewing man's mind, inspiring his spirit, and empowering his will.

It is into this tradition that we have come. We too should hear a different drummer. This will mean that there will be times when, if we are loyal to the truth, we will say what may disturb or upset our people and perhaps get us into trouble. Ernest Fremont Tittle said once: "The fellow who trims the truth makes a hit, while the one who tells the truth gets hit." [26] This means that the preacher must be a man of courage. When a minister is for any reason no longer able to say what he thinks or believes, his usefulness to God has been greatly impaired. It would be fortunate perchance could we always avoid controversial issues and practice the art of "living in safety zones," but it is not possible to do that. Once when Emerson was invited to lecture at the Salem Lyceum he was advised to choose his own subject "provided no allusions are made to religious controversy or other exciting topics upon which the public mind is honestly divided." He replied: "I am really sorry that

[26] Ralph Sockman, *Recoveries in Religion,* p. 110.

174

THE PREACHER AND THE TRUTH

any person in Salem should think me capable of accepting an invitation so incumbered." In his journal below this comment appears a quotation from the anecdotes of Lady Mary Montagu: "The motto on all palace gates is *Hush*." [27]

One needs courage especially in dealing with his friends. Sometimes it is easier to denounce the devil and all his works than to stand for the truth at the cost of hurting those who may be near and dear. It must have been easier for Jesus to withstand his enemies than to endure the misunderstandings with his family and friends which his loyalty to the truth made necessary. His remark to Peter has become a byword with us: "Get thee behind me, Satan" (Matt. 16:23). We repeat that so glibly that you might almost think the Master were wishing Peter a merry Christmas! Actually those words, addressed to his best friend, must have taken more courage than his denunciation of the Pharisees.

We need courage. Today's pastors are much more exposed to the hazards of war than those to whom Robert Louis Stevenson wrote the following words, yet they are still significant:

You pastors do not go to war; you must be braver-hearted, then, at home. The world has no room for cowards. We must all be ready somehow to toil, to suffer, to die. And yours is not the less noble because no drum beats before you, when you go out into your daily battlefields; and no crowds shout your coming, when you return from your daily victory or defeat.[28]

[27] Quoted by Arthur C. McGiffert, Jr., *Religion in Life*, Spring, 1939, p. 267.

[28] Graham Balfour, *Life of Stevenson*, p. 227.

Said Phillips Brooks:

V The timid minister is as bad as the timid surgeon. Courage is good everywhere, but it is necessary here. If you are afraid of men and a slave to their opinion, go and do something else. Go and make shoes to fit them. Go even and paint pictures which you know are bad but which suit their bad taste. But do not keep on all your life preaching sermons which shall say not what God sent you to declare, but what they hire you to say.[29]

I have suggested four marks of the workman who needs not be ashamed: industry, integrity, interest, independence. Perhaps all I have said might be summarized by saying that the man who is "approved unto God" is the man who knows God firsthand. What Thomas Carlyle said about his parish holds true of every parish. "What this parish needs before everything else," he said, "is a preacher who knows God otherwise than by hearsay." [30] Emerson made a similar observation. In a divinity school address he said that the primary duty of the preacher, without which his other attainments would be of questionable worth, was to "acquaint men first hand with Deity." [31] The crowning qualification of the workman who needs not be ashamed is that he is able to say with Paul: "I know whom I have believed" (II Tim. 1:12).

There are, speaking broadly, two kinds of knowledge— knowledge about and knowledge of. One is abstract, the other personal. One comes as information, the other as experience.

[29] Lectures on Preaching, p. 59.
[30] L. P. Jacks, Elemental Religion, p. 59.
[31] Addresses and Lectures, p. 146.

One is grasped by the mind, the other involves "all thy heart, and . . . all thy soul" as well (Matt. 22:37). In religion both kinds of knowledge are necessary, as I have said. For the Christian religion is not only a way of life but also a subject for study. Yet there can be little doubt that there is a big difference between being religiously informed and being Christian. The blind man whom Jesus healed knew surprisingly little about him. He surely would have failed miserably in a theological examination concerning the person of Christ. But he had the kind of knowledge which, from a Christian point of view, is of primary import. "One thing I know," he said, "that, whereas I was blind, now I see" (John 9:25). Christ had made all the difference to him between darkness and light. Wrote Hegel:

Were the knowledge of religion historical only we should have to regard theologians as resembling the bank-clerk who enters in his ledger large sums of money belonging to other people, yet acquires little of his own.[32]

But the knowledge of the Christian religion is far from being "historical only." Luther made this clear once in a striking epigram. Said he:

He who merely studies the commandments of God (*mandata Dei*) is not greatly moved. But he who listens to God commanding (*Deum mandantem*), how can he fail to be terrified by majesty so great? [33]

There can be no doubt that the knowledge that issues in

[32] H. R. Mackintosh, *Types of Modern Theology*, p. 2.
[33] J. S. Whale, *Christian Doctrine*, p. 151.

redemptive power, the knowledge that transforms and enriches life, is that which comes through firsthand acquaintance with, and experience of, the truth. Surely it was of this kind of knowledge the Master was thinking when he said: "Ye shall know the truth, and the truth shall make you free" (John 8: 32). Or, "Have I been so long time with you, and yet hast thou not known me, Philip?" (John 14:9). This kind of knowledge takes more discipline, more moral and spiritual effort than knowledge about. This is why as preachers our religious information tends to exceed our Christian experience. We need to remember, however, what William James once said about religion: "He who lives the life of it, however narrowly, is a better servant than he who merely knows about it, however much." [34]

In this connection let us recall a revealing incident in the book of the Acts. The seven sons of Sceva, a Jewish high priest, impressed by the mighty works of Paul, borrowed his religious formula and hoped that its parrotlike repetition would bring results. So they said to the evil spirits: "We adjure you by Jesus whom Paul preacheth" (19:13). But nothing happened. The formula was ineffective, it did not work. It is still true, and ever will be, that the repetition of pious phrases divorced from Christian conviction and experience is vain. The Jesus whom Paul preached was a tremendous power in the life of Paul. But he can never be a power in your life or mine until, like Paul, we too can say: "I know whom I have believed" (II Tim. 1:12). This is the knowledge that gives power.

[34] Quoted by Charles W. Gilkey, *Current Religious Thought*, February, 1948, p. 10.

It may be that our very familiarity with the language of our religion militates against such knowledge. This was the danger that Phillips Brooks pointed out long ago. You will recall he said that the preacher was in danger of becoming like a train crier, who calls out the stations all along the line to the travelers who board the train while he himself might not have visited one of them. "Take with you words," said Hosea (14:2). But anyone who knows that prophet will realize that his words were not echoes of what he had heard, picked up and repeated parrotlike, but bore the authentic marks of his own deep, if tragic, experience. Isaiah pronounces his woe upon those whose fear of the Lord "is a commandment of men which hath been taught them" (29:13 A.S.V.), as well he might. For it is only as the word becomes flesh, our flesh, dwells in us, only as in some real sense we too, like Paul, bear on our bodies the marks of the Lord Jesus, that our words will carry conviction and power. "Secondhand geography may be perfectly good geography. Secondhand faith is just not faith at all." [35]

The reason for this is clear. The preacher's task is to bring others to a knowledge of the truth that sets men free, and how can he mediate that truth save as he himself knows firsthand its transforming power? The preacher is more than a teacher. His duty is not only to inform but to inspire; not only to enlighten but to enliven; not only to give people a knowledge about Christian truth but to bring them to a saving knowledge of Christ the Truth. The commitment of life to Christ is his ultimate aim. He is a propagandist unashamed. He wants converts to the Christian cause. It is obvious that this goal can be

[35] John Baillie, *Roots of Religion in the Human Soul*, p. 65.

reached only by that preacher who knows God "otherwise than by hearsay."

The life of the apostles is instructive here. We are always astonished that men who seemingly had so little could have accomplished so much. One main reason was that they carried out the command of Christ when he said, "Ye shall be my witnesses" (Acts 1:8 A.S.V.). They were witnesses to the truth, not merely apologists for it. There is a difference. One does not need to belittle the work of the apologist. Indeed he has done yeoman service for the church. More than once in its long history has the truth of Christianity been threatened by quasi-philosophical systems like Gnosticism and Neoplatonism, by pagan forms of faith like Mithraism and Manichaeanism. Let no one belittle the labors of those workmen who "rightly dividing the word of truth" rendered indispensable service in defending the truth against such errors. Yet as important as has been, and still is, the work of the apologist, the testimony of the witness is more important still. It is the witness who has kept, and keeps, the fires of faith alight. For not by excellence of speech, nor by arguments, but by lives aglow with the transforming and redemptive power of truth did the apostles make their impress upon their age. "When they beheld the boldness of Peter and John . . . they took knowledge." (Acts 4:13 A.S.V.) "It has been truly said that the conquering power of the gospel was not in the arguments of Clement or Tertullian, sound as they were, but in the evidence of Christian life and love, Christian purity and patience." [36] It is beyond doubt true that the Christian church has been strongest when she has

[36] *An Outline of Christianity,* ed. F. J. Foakes-Jackson, II, 73.

placed the emphasis on testifying rather than on arguing. Or as Ambrose expressed it: "It was not by dialectic that it pleased God to save his people; for the kingdom of God consists in simplicity of faith, not in wordy contention." [37]

We should all be grateful and proud of the excellent intellectual training available for the modern minister. He can hold his own today against the sophisticated, and often go them one better. But this of itself is not enough. "It is good," declared Phillips Brooks, "to be a Herschel who describes the sun; but it is better to be a Prometheus who brings the sun's fire to the earth." [38] Paul was a learned man, and as I have said, our intellectual equipment in an age like this is imperative. Yet Paul was willing to become a fool for Christ's sake. He found that "the foolishness of God is wiser than men" (I Cor. 1:25). "And I, brethren," he writes, "when I came to you, came not with excellency of speech or of wisdom, declaring unto you the testimony of God. For I determined not to know any thing among you, save Jesus Christ, and him crucified.... And my speech and my preaching was not with enticing words of man's wisdom, but in demonstration of the Spirit and of power: that your faith should not stand in the wisdom of men, but in the power of God" (I Cor. 2:1-2, 4-5).

In these searching words we discover the secret of the apostles' effectiveness. Nineteen centuries of Christian history have made this an open secret. Without a firsthand knowledge of God in Christ the Christian minister, no matter how well educated and trained, is ill-equipped indeed. For his major task, as I have

[37] F. H. Dudden, *Life and Times of St. Ambrose*, II, 558.
[38] James S. Stewart, *Heralds of God*, p. 57.

said, is to bring others to know God, and it is difficult to see how he can perform this save as his own life bears evidence of that truth. The question of Jesus to Pilate has peculiar relevance for preachers: "Sayest thou this thing of thyself, or did others tell it thee of me?" (John 18:34). There is much in this world that we have to take on the say-so of others because we have not the ability, the equipment, nor the opportunity for firsthand investigation and knowledge. But in the good providence of God the knowledge of his nature, will, and purpose for mankind, as revealed in Christ, is withheld from no one who seeks in sincerity and truth.

I conclude as I began, by saying that the preacher is at his best when he is transmissive, when something happens to him or through him, rather than by him. "It is not the lofty sails but the unseen wind that moves the ship." [39] Such has been the experience of the greatest souls. "It is God which worketh in you," said Paul, "both to will and to do." (Phil. 2:13.) "The Father that dwelleth in me, he doeth the works," said the Master. (John 14:10.)

A few years ago one of the greatest missionaries of our age, C. F. Andrews, fell on sleep. He was commonly known as "C.F.A." It was Gandhi, I believe, who said the initials stood for "Christ's Faithful Apostle." A great tribute was once paid this modern apostle to India by a brilliant Hindu editor who said to Sherwood Eddy: "I have read little of the Bible but I have seen Christ in Andrews' life; and I would give anything to be like him." [40] You see, it was not Andrews but Christ in

[39] MacNeile Dixon, *The Human Situation*, p. 64.
[40] *Pathfinders of the World Missionary Crusade*, pp. 111-12.

Andrews that made Andrews the power that he was. From the days of the apostles men of faith have regarded themselves as but earthen vessels for the treasure of the divine truth. It will always be so.

At the conclusion of a service of worship at which a widely known preacher had poured out his soul, someone inquired: "And what did you think of him?"

"To tell the truth," came the reply, "I did not think of him. All through the service I kept thinking of his Master."

The workman of whom that can be said needs not to be ashamed.

VI

CHRIST THE TRUTH

WE have been considering truth in the abstract; now we confront it. "I am . . . the truth," said Jesus (John 14:6). This claim still stands after nineteen hundred years. During that period his life has been submitted to the most unrelenting, critical scrutiny. No life has undergone such thoroughgoing examination. No book in all the world has received such minute and merciless study as that which bears the record of his life. The New Testament has been scrutinized as if by a microscope. Yet we have found nothing to discredit this life. On the contrary the passing centuries have added to his stature. After nineteen hundred years his life still rings true.

Jesus' influence on history is unique. Kenneth Scott Latourette, in his revealing book *Anno Domini,* keeps repeating the phrase "the impulse from Jesus," as he points out the unparalleled influence that Jesus has exerted on our civilization. Is there any aspect of our culture that has not felt the impact of his life? Religion, education, music, literature, art, architecture, humanitarian and philanthropic movements, character-forming agencies—where would one begin or stop in trying to evaluate his influence? If we were to take out of our culture all that directly or indirectly derives from Jesus of Nazareth, what we should have left would resemble some Coventry or Cologne after the dive bombers had got through with it. Emerson was right when he said that the name of Jesus was not so much written as ploughed into history. "Jesus has had a more widespread effect upon individual men and upon human society than has any other who has ever appeared on the earth." [1]

We cannot explain this influence, however, by our customary methods of evaluation. The criteria we use in estimating greatness are wholly irrelevant when applied to him. This is evidenced when we remember the historical facts of his earthly ministry. They are most unimpressive. Consider some of these facts: the brevity of his life and singular brevity of his public career; that he left no written document; that he made no attempt to found an organization; and finally that he went down in the most ignominious sort of death, being crucified between two thieves. Any contemporary of our Lord with an eye to business simply could not from such scant, unpretentious facts have predicted any such world-wide, revolutionary effect as Jesus has had on history. The historic facts of his earthly life do not add up to any such result.

To account for Jesus' life, then, we are compelled to use some other measuring rod than we are wont to apply in making our historical judgments. There is more in him than meets the eye. "I have meat to eat that ye know not of." (John 4:32.) "The Father that dwelleth in me, he doeth the works." (John 14:10.) "With God all things are possible." (Matt. 19:26.) To say

---

[1] *Anno Domini,* pp. 7-8.

that with God all things are possible is another way of saying that with God the impossible has an embarrassing way of occurring. It did with Christ. "The stone which the builders rejected, the same is become the head of the corner." (Matt. 21:42.) His contemporaries could not explain him any more than can we. "Is not this the carpenter's son? is not his mother called Mary? and his brethren . . . and his sisters, are they not all with us? Whence then hath this man all these things?" (Matt. 13:55-56.)

The answer of the Christian church to that question, however phrased, has been in substance that Christ is the embodiment of Reality. There is that in the nature of man, as man responds to him, and that in the very nature of the universe whose laws unquestionably support his way of life, which conspire to give him his unique place in history—"far above . . . every name that is named" (Eph. 1:21). The apostle John, in speaking of the Master, said, "We beheld his glory, the glory as of the only begotten of the Father, full of grace and truth" (John 1:14). Jesus said of himself: "I am the . . . truth" (John 14:6). That explains his place in history.

Mark you, he did not say "I am a fact," as though he were appealing to the scientific mind; nor did he say "I present facts," as though he were appealing to the historians or jurists of the ages. He did not say "I speak the truth," as a moralist might have done; nor "I announce the truth," as a prophet would. He said: "I am the . . . truth," or perhaps more accurately, "I am truth." Jesus is the embodiment of Reality, his life a revelation of the nature and purpose of the living God. It is on that assumption that the Christian church finds the explana-

186

tion of his unique place in history. None other is adequate.

Now there are two very simple questions we ought to ask regarding this assertion of Jesus, "I am the truth." The first: "What kind of truth?" The second: "The truth about what?" First, then, of what kind of truth is Christ the embodiment? The answer is personal truth, by which I mean truth mediated through personality. In Christ we confront truth not in an abstract proposition or logical deduction, as in philosophy; not truth in a formula or in a law, as in science; but truth in a life, truth in personality. At the center of our religion we confront not a dogma or doctrine, not a theoretical, legalistic, or theological proposition, not a book or an organization, but a person, a life—"the Word was made flesh" (John 1:14). This fact may be oversimplified but it cannot be overemphasized. It cannot be overemphasized because it is one unique mark of Christianity. Consider now the difference in this regard between Christianity and other religions.

Take Buddhism. Gautama, the Buddha, although he claimed to be superior to the gods, who, he insisted, stood in need of salvation from suffering like ordinary mortals, never countenanced nor encouraged worship of himself. He never said: "Come unto me, for I am the truth." He announced a saving truth which man had to grasp for himself as best he could. He spoke of truth under the simile of a drug which one might use efficaciously without any reference on the part of the patient to him who discovered or prescribed it. Hence his doctrine and his order—his order of monks, the Sangha—were independent of his person. The doctrine, not the person, is the central fact of Buddhism. Said Buddha:

Somebody, O mendicants, is following me holding the edge of my garment . . . but he is far from me and I am far from him. Why? Because he has not seen the Doctrine; and not having seen the Doctrine, he does not see me either. Somebody lives at a distance of 100 yojanas. . . . He is close to me and I am close to him. Why? Because he has seen the Doctrine, and having seen the Doctrine he has seen me. . . . The one that hath seen the Doctrine hath seen me.[2]

When the Buddha lay dying his beloved Ananda, the John of his disciple band, wept. But the Buddha consoled him:

It may be, Ananda, that some of you will think, "the word of The Teacher is a thing of the past; we have now no Teacher." But that, Ananda, is not the correct view. The Doctrine . . . and the Discipline, . . . which I have taught and enjoined upon you, is to be your teacher when I am gone.[3]

So where the Buddha says, "He that hath seen the Doctrine hath seen me," Christ says, "He that hath seen me hath seen the Father" (John 14:9). That within a century or two of his death the Buddha was being deified by his followers suggests that personality, and only personality with cosmic connotation, is the answer to the questing spirit of man.

So too Islam. Mohammed laid claim to no special significance of himself. He said he was just a man like other men. An old tradition has Mohammed say: "Praise me not as Jesus, the Son of Mary, was praised." [4] Any idea of incarnation was considered

[2] Nathan Söderblom, *The Living God*, p. 325.
[3] *Ibid.*
[4] *Ibid.*, p. 327.

heretical by Islam. The most holy and abiding thing Mohammed had to offer his people was a book—the Koran. Jesus, on the contrary, "closed the book . . . and sat down." And he said, "This day is this scripture fulfilled in your ears" (Luke 4:20-21). Fulfilled in a life, a personality.

This failure to identify truth with personality is found too among Greek teachers. Socrates once said to his followers: "You, if you take my advice, will think little about Socrates but a great deal about truth." Not so Jesus. "I am the . . . truth," he said. "Follow me"; "Learn of me"; "Come unto me." In comparing Jesus with Socrates, Phillips Brooks writes:

> They start from different points. They journey by different roads. They come in sight of one another when their separate journeys mount to their highest elevations. They travel in the same direction, but they do not travel together. The one reveals; the other argues.[5]

If Jesus placed his personality at the center, rather than his teaching, it was because his teaching was so completely embodied in his personality. He is unique among all religious teachers in that he was what he said. As he preached, so he practiced. His life was the complete embodiment of his message. No other religious teacher in history has ever so impressed his followers as completely embodying what he taught. It is impossible, therefore, to separate what he said from what he was. In literal truth, "the Word was made flesh" (John 1:14).

Now from this fact that the truth of our religion is truth in a person, in a life, two results obtain. For one thing, if Christian truth is truth in a life, then it follows that to know Chris-

[5] *The Influence of Jesus*, p. 48.

tian truth we must know the life who incarnates it. We can know a theorem of Euclid without knowing Euclid, or some biological truth like the circulation of the blood without establishing any personal relationship with William Harvey. But is it possible really to know Christian truth without knowing Christ? The apostles would have said no to that question. They did not go out to preach the Sermon on the Mount or the Golden Rule or the principles of Jesus as abstractions. They were not concerned primarily with "the Jesus way of life." Their primary interest was Jesus himself. They resolved "not to know anything among you, save Jesus Christ, and him crucified" (I Cor. 2:2). "We preach Christ crucified." (I Cor. 1:23.) That was their gospel. And that must be our gospel too —the heart of it.

This coming to know Christ is what makes Christian truth redemptive truth, the truth that transforms, not just the truth that informs. The task of the educator is to inform the uninstructed. The task of the minister begins with instruction but it does not end there. For the truth we proclaim aims not only at informing minds but at changing lives. By this truth we are not only enlightened but enlivened. This is because Christian truth is truth in a life. Men are informed by ideas, but they are redeemed by the contagion of personality. "That I may know him," said Paul, "and the power of his resurrection, and the fellowship of his sufferings . . . if by any means I might attain unto the resurrection of the dead." (Phil. 3:10-11.) The death to which Paul here refers is physical, but there was another kind of death from which Christ delivered Paul—the death that was the wage of sin. "O wretched man that I am! who shall deliver me from the body of this death?" (Rom. 7:24.) "The law of the Spirit of life in Christ Jesus hath made me free from the law of sin and death." (Rom. 8:2.) Paul broke with the law because it lacked transforming power. "What the law could not do, . . . God sending his own Son" (Rom. 8:3) accomplished. To know the law and to know Christ were to Paul quite different. The latter was redemptive knowledge, knowledge of a person. "I live; yet not I, but Christ liveth in me: and the life which I now live in the flesh I live by the faith of the Son of God, who loved me, and gave himself for me." (Gal. 2:20.) "I know *whom* I have believed" (II Tim. 1:12)—not *what*.

Christian truth, then, is redemptive truth because it requires not simply knowledge about something but knowledge of someone. It is personal. As James Bissett Pratt has written: "I suppose, no other one thing has ever been such a power for the moral transformation of life as the experience of falling in love with Jesus." [6] This is the heart of Christianity: not simply correct views of doctrine, nor orthodox views of the Bible, not the meticulous performance of ecclesiastical rites—these are secondary. The heart of Christianity is love for, loyalty to, and so knowledge of, a person. To know Christ, our sins in the light of his purity, our possibilities in the light of his achievement, God's forgiving love and grace in the light of his passion, to strive by God's help to become more like Christ, to "press toward the mark for the prize of the high calling of God in Christ Jesus" (Phil. 3:14)—that is the heart of Christianity.

[6] *Hibbert Journal*, April, 1936, p. 425.

But truth in a life is not only redemptive; it is also living, developing, growing truth. Now of course all truth is alive in the sense that all truth is relevant. The truth that two plus two makes four, or that the angles at the base of an isosceles triangle are equal, though not exciting, is not dead because it is relevant. It will be admitted, however, that the truth incarnated in a life suggests a vitality incomparably greater than truth expressed in an axiom or formula, especially in such a life as that of the Master. H. G. Wells, in mentioning the three men whom he regarded as the greatest in history, said that the historian's test of an individual's greatness is "What did he leave to grow? Did he start men to thinking along fresh lines with a vigor that persisted after him?" "By this test," he concludes, "Jesus stands first." [7] The opposition to Jesus' public ministry, resulting in his crucifixion, grew essentially out of the difference between the truth in him—living, dynamic, developing truth—and truth in the Pharisaic law, static and inert.

That Jesus thought of truth as possessing a dynamic quality, inspiring men to growing and expanding insights, is evident. He said as much: "I have yet many things to say unto you, but ye cannot bear them now. Howbeit when he, the Spirit of truth, is come, he will guide you into all truth: . . . and he will show you things to come." (John 16:12-13.) "Greater works than these shall he do." (John 14:12.) That this spirit was directly contrary to the teaching of the Pharisees is evident. "A Midrash on Deuteronomy says plainly, 'No other Moses will come and bring another law for there is no law left in

[7] *Reader's Digest,* May, 1935, p. 13.

heaven.' " [8] Jesus, however, thought differently. "Ye have heard that it was said by them of old time, . . . but I say unto you." (Matt. 5:21, 22.) These were the words of an adventurous spirit who believed that the living God had not spoken his last word. Jesus' view of truth was dynamic and that of the Pharisees static. The Pharisees believed that the law contained God's complete and final revelation. In it God had spoken his last word. He had nothing else to say. Jesus did not believe that. The God who had spoken in times past was the living God and had yet many things to say.

The Pharisees did not think so. They were traditionalists in the bad sense. They worshiped the letter and so betrayed the spirit of the past. The difference between Jesus and the Pharisees was that to them the past was a hitching post; to him a guidepost. To them tradition was a swimming pool in which they lolled about; to him a springboard, its choicest values providing the incentive to further discovery in the spirit of the living God who leads men as fast as they will follow into a fuller knowledge of his living truth. Jesus warned against sewing new cloth on old garments, and said that the new wine could not be contained within the old wineskins. He saw incomparable values in tradition, but to him the wise scribe was he who would bring out of his treasure things *new* and old. This conflict between Jesus and the Pharisees proved irreconcilable. Here, if ever, an irresistible force met an immovable object. The result was a cross. From Jesus' day to our own, tradition has tended to thwart and crucify the truth. What Jesus said to the Pharisees he could have repeated down the ages

[8] Harvey Branscomb, *Jesus and the Law of Moses*, p. 27.

even until now: "Ye made the commandment of God of none effect by your tradition" (Matt. 15:6).[9]

This conflict between the traditionalists and the pioneers, between those whose view of truth was static rather than dynamic, did not begin with Jesus any more than it ended with him. Consider an incident from the book of Zechariah. The Israelites, after a long exile, returned to Jerusalem, intent on rebuilding their beloved city. A young man, young in years only and so not necessarily young, was seen mulling about the old foundations, measuring rod in hand, intent on building the new city according to the exact pattern of the old. But Zechariah, older perhaps in years but young in outlook and spirit, and so young, stopped him. This new Jerusalem, so Zechariah thought, was not to be modeled after the traditional one. The old one had been fortified. The very formidableness of its fortifications had invited attack. The new Jerusalem, on the contrary, was to be like a series of open villages. "Be not like your fathers," said Zechariah. (1:3 Moffatt.) That is to say, do not just copy them slavishly. Put aside your measuring rods and be true to the fathers by incarnating their spirit.

Who could possibly estimate the appalling wrong that has been done, and still is being done, to truth, living dynamic truth, by these miserable measuring rods by which we try to impose on a new age, with its new problems and possibilities, the cramping and too often utterly inadequate dimensions of another day. The most distressing part of the whole business is that these "young men" with their measuring rods honestly

[9] There was a liberal element in Pharisaism, nearer, no doubt, to the Master's point of view, but it was a minority group.

feel that in the slavish imitation of their fathers they are being loyal to them. Precisely the opposite is the case. Sometimes we are never so unlike our ancestors as when we try hardest to copy them slavishly. James Truslow Adams, in speaking of the Daughters of the American Revolution, writes:

Considering the extreme die-hard conservatism of the resolutions of the "Daughters of the Revolution" today, it seems impossible to avoid the conclusion that very few of them would have been Mothers of the Revolution in 1776, when revolution meant riding the whirlwind of social disorder.[10]

This group, however, need not be singled out. These women are not the only ones who, in trying to be loyal to the letter of tradition, betray the spirit of the past. It is not only they who fail to understand that more often than not the very fathers they revere were the radicals, the pioneers and adventurers of their generation, and that therefore to be true to them is not to stand where they stood but where they would stand were they alive today. Is it not right here we often fail? "The task of statesmanship," said William Ewart Gladstone, "is to discover where God Almighty is going during the next fifty years." [11] But a statesmanship that identifies patriotism with a slavish imitation of the past, and fails to realize that "new occasions teach new duties" will never measure up to the demands of its day and generation.

For example, at the close of World War I there were indications enough as to where God Almighty was going and was

[10] *Epic of America*, p. 92.
[11] *Riverside Church Monthly*, Summer, 1946, p. 127.

urging us to go. Those who had eyes to see could read his righteous judgments in the debris of a world whose pagan concepts
of power and wholly unchristian competitive nationalism had
contributed so largely to its downfall. If ever God commanded
men to move out into an ampler life of international co-operation, he did then. The time was ripe for it. But the nations
said "No," and in that answer our nation's voice was the loud-
est. The United States, founded by brave adventurers and developed by hardy pioneers: that we of all people should have
taken our measuring rods and insisted that the new world be
built on the same dimensions as the old is a clear indication
of how we betray the truth through blind, misguided loyalty.
Are we not reaping now, in the grim aftermath of World War
II, the unspeakable tragedy of that appalling blunder? Tradition, then, when it evokes a blind, uncritical loyalty, is one of
the greatest enemies of the truth. There is nothing more dangerous than to stand still when God says "Move on." As George
Buttrick puts it, "In God 'we live and move'—and if we do
not move we cannot live." [12]

Not only in the field of politics, however, but also in the field
of religion have measuring rods been an enemy of the living,
dynamic truth which Christ has revealed.

> All our fathers have been Churchmen,
>   Nineteen hundred years or so,
> And to every new suggestion
>   They have always answered No.[13]

[12] *Jesus Came Preaching*, p. 62.
[13] *Riverside Church Monthly*, Summer, 1946, p. 127.

Sometimes of course they should have, for the new is not always the true. More often than not, however, our misguided loyalty to the letter of the law has been a millstone about the neck of the truth as it is in Jesus. Take but one of scores of examples. Witness the conflict between Galileo and the church of his day. Aristotle had taught that bodies of different weights would fall through the air at different speeds. He was mistaken. He taught that the earth was the center of the universe. He was mistaken. He said there were 1,027 stars in the sky. In this too he was far from right. These and similar beliefs of the philosopher had been incorporated in the teaching of the Roman Catholic Church. Galileo proved that they were false. After he had invented his telescope he invited the powers that be to look through it and see the heavens which Aristotle never saw. The reply was:

"Listen, Galileo! The science of the world was built on the pillars of Aristotelian wisdom. For two thousand years men have lived and died in the belief that the earth is the center of the universe and man the lord of it. . . . All that we know today, from logic to medicine, from botany to astronomy, is Christian and Aristotelian. . . . Leave me my peace of mind! I refuse to look into that tube!"

"But the truth, Cesare! The truth! Doesn't that mean anything?" cried Galileo.

"No, I need my peace and happiness!" [14]

It was no fault of the church that this honest-minded Italian escaped martyrdom. Many did not. Are there any pages of history more smirched with infamy than those written by men

[14] Zsolt de Harsanyi, *The Star-Gazer*, p. 282.

who, in the name of Christ the Truth, have persecuted, tortured, and killed the brave souls through whom God sought to speak his surer word and reveal his clearer light? Even today, though happily the methods of the Inquisition are a thing of the past, does not the cause of truth still often suffer more severely at the hands of its would-be defenders than its enemies? Might we now be attaching to some dogma or ecclesiastical policy or procedure the same kind of finality the Pharisees did to the law? Jesus said: "I am the way." (John 14:6.) The way suggests motion. Dean Willard Sperry reminds us that down the centuries men have taken theological snapshots of Christ the Way. But men forget that while the picture is static the life moves on, and so tend to identify a theological picture taken in the third, fourth, or fifth century with the Christ of today. This is an unfortunate mistake. For the truth that is in Jesus is not the truth of a formula or of a dogma. It is truth in a life, and this life, though "the same yesterday, and today, and for ever" (Heb. 13:8), may mean something new and different, yea, more, to the on-going generations.

It is not that the truth about Jesus changes. It is rather that men, as they face the changed conditions peculiar to their day and generation, may interpret it differently. The theological garments Christ wore at Nicea in the third century, or Chalcedon in the fifth, may not mean to us what they did to men of that age. This does not mean at all that Christ has lost his appeal or pre-eminence. For this is the glorious fact about Christianity: its truth is perennial. Its truth is not a static law but a vital principle amenable to endless variations and applications. The literalists therefore who insist on the letter of the truth do most tragically betray the spirit of it. As Alfred North Whitehead, the philosopher, says: "Those societies which cannot combine reverence for their symbols with freedom of revision must ultimately decay either from anarchy or from the slow atrophy of a life stifled by useless shadows." [15] E. Stanley Jones, the evangelist, expresses the same truth in striking language when he says,

The Word is greater than our words. Hence our creeds must be eternally open on the side of revision—revision toward larger, fuller meanings. A fixed creed becomes a false creed. For Christ is forever beyond us, calling us to new meanings and new surrenders and new adventures.[16]

Now we come to the second question. If Christ be the truth, then we must ask not only "What kind of truth?" but also "The truth about what?" And the answer must be that since, as we have said, Christ is personal truth, it follows that he must be the truth about persons. That is to say, truth in a life is truth about life—"I am the way, the truth, and the life" (John 14:6). The truth God reveals in Christ is not about rocks or stars or atoms. It is not about any *thing* whatsoever. It is truth about man himself.

This is the most important truth we could possibly have. For until man faces the truth about himself, comes to know the ultimate meaning of his life in the scheme of things, the values, principles, goals that are worthy of his striving, then his knowledge of all else, however vast, is of questionable worth. It is

[15] Harold Bosley, *Main Issues Confronting Christendom*, p. 62.
[16] *The Way*, p. 54.

BEARING WITNESS TO THE TRUTH

only as he knows the truth about himself that his other knowledge can be used to further his best interests rather than to has-
ten his downfall and destruction. Is not this in a word the problem of modern man? He knows nature but does not know himself. He has mastered nature but has not achieved self-mastery.
It is precisely because man's knowledge of nature has so far
outstripped his knowledge of himself that he now lives in constant fear of being destroyed by the devices of his own creation. As Edmund W. Sinnott of Yale University, writes:

No social mechanism, no economic system, can save us now, . . .
not unless man himself can be improved, can be exalted far above
the beast he was, can any social order now survive. Whether we
relish it or not, here we must deal with spirit as well as mind.[17]

Our lot now has become peculiarly precarious because our
penetrating knowledge of nature has led us, unhappily perchance, to discover one of nature's ultimate secrets—atomic
fission. We are frankly afraid. And those who are best informed
are most apprehensive—the scientists. The basic trouble of
course is that our knowledge of nature has outstripped our
knowledge of ourselves. We have learned how to release atomic
energy but are the utmost novices in dealing with the moral
and spiritual forces within ourselves. That is to say we are ex-
ceedingly well informed about things but are in the dark about
ourselves. What we really fear, though we never say so, is not
atomic energy but human treachery. We are untamed. A small
boy, when asked "What is the most dangerous part of an auto-

[17] "Science and the Whole Man," *American Scientist*, January, 1948, p. 136.

mobile?" wisely replied, "The driver!" That is where our real trouble lies. The only way we can keep our knowledge of the world outside of us from destroying us is by increasing our knowledge of the world inside of us; that is to say, in coming to know the truth about ourselves. As someone has said: "We have learned in airplanes to fly through the air like birds, and in submarines to swim under the sea like fish. All that remains for us is to learn to walk the earth like men."

That is what Jesus came to teach us. He came, the truth in a life, to reveal the truth about life. He came, the truth made in the fashion of a man, to reveal the truth about man. "He knew what was in man." (John 2:25.) It is revealing to see how many current books on psychology, in pointing the way out, come up with some Christian insight which Jesus in untechnical phraseology hit upon long ago. This, I suppose, is partly due to the fact that most of our mental difficulties are moral and spiritual in their origin. Truly Jesus knew what was in man. The path to a healthy mind, to inner peace, was blazed long ago by him who is indeed "the true Light, which lighteth every man that cometh into the world" (John 1:9). He is the truth about man.

I propose now, in barest outline, to suggest what seems to me to be the heart of that truth as it affects human life and destiny. I shall mention four of the insights of Jesus concerning human life which, to my knowledge, no one has ever stressed as did he. Certainly in no one else have they assumed the winsomeness, appeal, or social significance they have in him. The first of these insights I have come to regard as basic because the other three derive from it, and but for it would be largely deprived of their meaning.

This basic insight, however phrased, is that the deepest reality of life is spiritual, and that therefore spiritual values are primary and definitive. In how many and varied ways did Jesus teach this! He was always insisting that the treasures most to be desired are not the material ones laid up on earth, subject to decay or loss, but the spiritual ones laid up in heaven and so abiding. Material things are of great value, to be sure, because man needs them. That is why God provided them. Jesus therefore taught us to pray for daily bread. But man does not live by bread alone. His life does not consist in the abundance of the things he possesses. The life is more than meat. If therefore we prosper materially, pull down our barns and build greater, even to the extent of gaining the whole world, but in the process lose our souls, we are fools. For our souls are ourselves, we are spirits. And what does it profit if in possessing everything we lose the one possession which gives meaning to all else? Therefore "seek ye first the kingdom of God, and his righteousness; and all these things shall be added unto you" (Matt. 6:33).

Jesus believed in the importance of the body. Much of his ministry was given to healing the sick. But he insisted that the body is not an end in itself. It is the habitation of the spirit and must be made subservient thereto. The prodigal who selfishly takes what he regards as his own and goes off to indulge his lusts is not on the road to life but death. For man, being essentially a spiritual being, never finds himself in his undisciplined hours. Therefore if your hand or foot offend you, get rid of it. It is better to enter into life maimed than to miss it whole. Avoid therefore the broad way which leads to destruction and choose the straight and narrow way, which, through the disciplining of the flesh, clarifies and enhances the values of the spirit. Jesus went so far as to say that if one's loyalty to spiritual values exposed him to physical peril, he should have no fear. "Fear not them which kill the body, but are not able to kill the soul." (Matt. 10:28.) Rather fear God and the destruction of the soul.

Because man is essentially a spiritual being his basic problems, as the Master teaches implicitly, are not economic, political, or social but moral and spiritual. No economic, political, or social arrangement that violates some basic moral principle of justice or righteousness can possibly work effectively. Never mind how beautiful the superstructure, if the foundation be insecure or rotten the structure cannot last. "Look, teacher, what a size these stones and buildings are!" Jesus said to him, "You see these great buildings? Not a stone shall be left on another, without being torn down." (Mark 13:1-2 Moffatt.) It is only as we build the house of civilization on the rock of truth that it will withstand the storms, the strains and stresses that arise. If we build on anything less than moral and spiritual truth—wood, hay, stubble—the day will declare it. The wise man therefore puts his house upon the rock of truth—spiritual truth.

The Master would say too that since the basic fact of life is moral and spiritual, the only ultimately effective weapons of one's warfare are moral and spiritual weapons. For our wrestling is "not against flesh and blood, but . . . against spiritual wickedness" (Eph. 6:12)—the hosts of evil. Force, therefore, being a material entity, can never possibly provide the final solution of any human problem. It is not wholly out of place in God's plan; but its place as a final resource is wholly inadequate. For though force can drive the money-changers out of the temple, it cannot drive avarice and greed out of the money-changers, and until this spiritual task is accomplished they will return again and again. This inner spiritual evil therefore must be attacked by spiritual weapons. Love, persuasion, the appeal to reason, the cultivating of understanding, the growth of good will—in these spiritual weapons, however inept we may be in using them, lie the one hope of man's eventual progress. For man is a soul, a spirit, and only as he begins to comprehend the nature of spiritual values and to put those first will he find the road to the abundant life which God intends.

Such, though briefly and inadequately summarized, is in substance what we may regard as the basic, over-all emphasis of Jesus on the essentially spiritual nature of reality.

A second insight of the Master is the supreme worth and dignity of the individual. This follows. For since spiritual values are primary, and since these values exist only in the individual, it follows that this fact gives supreme worth and dignity to the individual. Whether it is spiritual values that give supreme meaning to personality, or personality that makes the values supreme, is unimportant. The fact is that God has joined them together and that separated each is meaningless.

The coming into his own of the person, the shaking loose of the individual from the group, is one of the interesting developments of our religion. In early Judaism it was not the

204

individual but the group which was regarded as the primary unit. Perhaps the first step in giving the person his rightful place was taken by Ezekiel, who declared God would deal with individuals each on his own merit—"The soul that sinneth, it shall die" (18:4). A more significant step was made by Jeremiah, who saw more clearly than did Ezekiel the significance of the individual as a religious unit. "O Jehovah, thou knowest; remember me, and visit me. . . . Thy words were found, and I did eat them; and thy words were unto me a joy and the rejoicing of my heart. . . . O Jehovah, my strength, and my stronghold, and my refuge in the day of affliction." (15:15-16; 16:19 A.S.V.) Jesus, however, goes further still. The individual is of supreme value to him, not because, as with Ezekiel, God condemns or acquits us one by one; nor even because, as with Jeremiah, God knows us one by one; but rather because each individual is precious in God's sight, precious because of his peculiar kinship as a spiritual being to God, his Creator and Father. His three parables, the lost sheep, the lost coin and, supremely, the lost son, illustrate this. "It is not the will of your Father who is in heaven, that one of these little ones should perish." (Matt. 18:14.)

This Christian concept of our value as derived solely from our relationship to God is many a sea mile from the secular concept of the worth of the individual as propounded by such thinkers as Comte or John Dewey, who seem to find something intrinsically valuable in the individual as such. Actually, apart from his relationship to God, there is nothing in the individual which in the long run makes him any more intrinsically valuable than any other animal, since without God both in the long run share the same fate. This is why Harnack is right in saying, "Jesus Christ was the first to bring the value of every human soul to light," [18] an insight which C. E. M. Joad calls "the greatest gift of Christianity to the world." [19]

A third major insight of Jesus, which follows from what I have termed his basic teaching, is his emphasis on brotherhood or community. This follows logically. For the quality that makes any individual of value—his relationship to God— makes every individual of value, since every individual is potentially a child of God. The value of each individual therefore is an inherent one and derives from his worth as a child of God, regardless of the accident of birth, station, or nation. What therefore makes one man inherently valuable makes all men so, since all are children of God. This means that the walls which pride, ignorance, or prejudice build are broken down, and individuals are lifted clear and viewed in the all-encompassing light of children of the God and Father of us all, who "hath made of one blood all nations of men for to dwell on all the face of the earth" (Acts 17:26). This explains the Master's revolutionary concept that we are all members of a family, the family of God, and so members one of another.

Jesus taught this by rejecting the title "Son of David" and choosing instead "Son of man." He taught it by refusing to help restore the kingdom of Israel, a kingdom that was essentially nationalistic, and proclaiming instead the Kingdom of God, a frontierless kingdom to which men would come from

[18] Quoted by Harry Emerson Fosdick, A Guide to Understanding the Bible, p. 72.
[19] Quoted by John Baillie, Invitation to Pilgrimage, p. 127.

the east and west, bound in a spiritual kinship which transcends every barrier. He taught it by bravely breaking through the barriers of race and class and bringing Samaritans, Syrophoenicians, Romans, publicans, and sinners within his fellowship. In these and other ways he taught that men are all members of God's family. "Whosoever shall do the will of my Father, . . . the same is my brother." (Matt. 12:50.) This too brought him into heated conflict with his contemporaries, whose racial and nationalistic pride made the truth of universalism anathema.

A fourth teaching of Jesus is his emphasis on inwardness. Men are not to be judged by their outward acts merely but by their inner motives. This too grows out of what I have called his basic teaching. For since man is essentially a spiritual being then obviously it is not what a man does but the spirit, the motive, in which he does it that reveals the true character of the man. A seemingly good deed, if prompted by an unworthy motive, is, according to Jesus, not a good deed. Similarly the evil in an evil deed is not in the deed but in the motive. The sin in murder is not in the act but in the impulse of hate that prompts it. So too it is not the act that makes the man an adulterer but the lustful look which makes one commit "adultery in his heart." Perhaps one reason why the Master says we should not judge is that we often cannot know what is back of a man's actions, be they good or evil, and not knowing the motive we cannot know the man.

Consider now the bearing of this emphasis of Jesus on truth. Why did Christ the Truth put the emphasis upon inner motive rather than outward act? For two reasons, I think. First, a man who outwardly by his act says one thing while inwardly he intends another, is a man who lacks sincerity. Jesus' word for it was hypocrisy. He is like a counterfeit coin. He looks genuine but he is not. He does not ring true. The truth is not in him. This was in part the heart of Jesus' conflict with the Pharisees. Many of them were not what they seemed to be. They were actors, playing a part. "Woe unto you, scribes and Pharisees, hypocrites! . . . Ye are like unto whited sepulchres, which indeed appear beautiful outward. . . . Even so ye also outwardly appear righteous unto men, but within ye are full of hypocrisy and iniquity." (Matt. 23:27-28.) Such a spirit makes the discovery or experience of truth impossible. "Blessed are the pure in heart: for they shall see God." (Matt. 5:8.) None of us is pure enough; in this sense most of us "see through a glass, darkly" (I Cor. 13:12). But the fact is that the degree to which we apprehend eternal truth is measured by our sincerity.

In the second place, by his emphasis on the inner life Jesus pointed up that aspect of reality where man most surely meets the God of truth. It was not for nought that the psalmist prayed: "Search me, O God, and know my heart: try me, and know my thoughts" (139:23). "Cleanse thou me from secret faults." (19:12.) It is a truism that as a man thinketh in his heart, so is he. Our actions reflect our thoughts as surely as does a mirror our face. Redemption is from the inside out. The waters of life can never be clean if the inner springs are fouled. And only God can cleanse the inner springs. This was precisely the truth which many of the Pharisees overlooked. They so lived that men would applaud their outward acts, not so God would approve their inner motives. They loved the spotlight or lime-

208

light better than the sunlight. Hence Jesus' words: "Take heed that ye do not your alms before men, to be seen of them: otherwise ye have no reward of your Father who is in heaven" (Matt. 6:1).

It is therefore to the Father who sees in secret, who looks not at the outward appearance but at the heart and understands our thoughts afar off, that one brings his inner life, as he seeks cleansing and renewal. One who is more concerned that men shall approve his outward acts than God his inner motives will not know the truth. An act whose primary concern is the applause or approval of men is not likely to advance the truth. In Christ the Truth the reverse often occurred—his outward acts were condemned by men while the hidden motives were approved by God. Jesus' emphasis on inwardness therefore relates to truth, not only because it points to the singleness of purpose by which the truth is known but also because it brings one to the Father who seeth in secret. "Thou God seest me." (Gen. 16:13.) When a man believes that and so tries to

> Stand approved in sight of God
> Though worlds judge thee perverse [20]

he becomes a living symbol of the truth.

I have mentioned four of the insights of Jesus related to our lives. First, the primacy of spiritual values; second, the supreme worth and dignity of the individual; third, that we are members one of another and belong to the family of God; and final-

[20] Author unknown.

ly, that inner motive, not outward act, is the real measure of man.

If we have rightly interpreted the mind of the Master in this matter then it follows that these insights must bear some relationship to what is unquestionably the heart of his message, namely, his preaching of the Kingdom of God. He was awakened to his mission by the preaching of John the Baptist, who came saying: "Repent ye: for the kingdom of heaven is at hand" (Matt. 3:2). "Now after that John was put in prison, Jesus came into Galilee, preaching the gospel of the kingdom of God." (Mark 1:14.) The first petition of the prayer he taught us is "Thy kingdom come." Were one to select from all the teachings of Jesus one phrase which would most adequately summarize his concept of reality, would it not have to be "the Kingdom of God"? In that phrase lies hidden the truth about life as the Master conceived it.

The very mention of the phrase raises more questions than can be answered. Even competent New Testament scholars differ as to the implications of the phrase. Unless, however, that which meant so much to the Master is to be completely devoid of meaning for us, which would be tragic, we ought to be able to know whether the direction in which mankind is moving at any given period is toward or away from the ideals of the Kingdom. How can we intelligently pray "Thy kingdom come" if we have no idea of what we are praying for? How can our endeavor have any Christian meaning if we do not know whether our actions at any given time may be retarding or hastening the blessed day when the will of God shall be done on earth as it is in heaven? Or must Jesus say of us as he did of his contemporaries: "Ye can discern the face of the sky; but can ye not discern the signs of the times?" (Matt. 16:3).

Now the four insights of the Master that I have mentioned do give some social and ethical meaning to the burden of his teaching about the Kingdom of God. For that Kingdom is a spiritual rather than a material state—"My kingdom is not of this world" (John 18:36). In it personal values, personality, will be given primary consideration—"Whosoever shall offend one of these little ones" (Mark 9:42). As that Kingdom comes, the walls which now separate man from his brother——racial, social, economic, and national—and so destroy community, will be broken down. For in that Kingdom "there is neither Jew nor Greek, . . . ye are all one" (Gal. 3:28). The inner life, spirit and motive, will be the test—"the kingdom of God is within you" (Luke 17:21).

It is as we understand the truth of these insights of Jesus that we see more clearly into the nature of sin. Sin is a betrayal of such insights as we have mentioned. Whenever, to gain some material advantage we betray some spiritual truth, sell our brightright for a mess of pottage, we sin. Whenever we treat human personality as though it were a tool to be used and discarded, rather than as an object of intrinsic worth and dignity, we sin. Whenever we violate the spirit of community, and by our actions destroy the fellowship which is potential and God expects us to make actual, we sin. Whenever we use some outward or visible act as a cloak for our sinister and deceptive designs, we sin.

And sin brings its own punishment. The tragic and perilous condition of the world today should prove even to the most unimaginative that in disregarding these profound insights we bring havoc upon ourselves. These are the spiritual laws of God—the universe supports them. To work with them is to find life, to oppose them is to court disaster. In his letter to the Corinthians, Paul writes: "For other foundation can no man lay than that is laid, which is Jesus Christ. Now if any man build upon this foundation gold, silver, precious stones, wood, hay, stubble; every man's work shall be made manifest: for the day shall declare it" (I Cor. 3:11-13). How the day is declaring the truth of these insights of Jesus! Is it not now clear that they are not beautiful bubbles on the surface of reality but are reality itself, verified in the flaming crucible of life? They came as strange and unfamiliar sounds to the ears of his generation. They may seem strange even to the ears of some moderns. But the day is declaring their truth, for time is on the side of Christ the Truth and reveals the validity of his message in the vast and varied context of history and experience.

How could we doubt, for example, that the master key to life unlocks, as he taught, the door of spiritual reality? "True politics," said Kant, "cannot take a single step forward unless it has first done homage to morals." But this observation holds not only for politics but for every single human relationship. Man is a spiritual being living in a moral universe, he is free to do anything he likes except escape the moral consequences of his deeds. Neither his cleverness nor amazing technical skill can save him from such consequences as his precarious and tragic condition today eloquently testifies. Writes James Anthony Froude:

212

One lesson, and only one, history may be said to repeat with distinctness: that the world is built somehow on moral foundations; that in the long run it is well with the good; in the long run it is ill with the wicked.[21]

Is not life too verifying the Master's teaching concerning the value of the individual? It may be hard to define progress, but one thing is certain: any step that is really a step forward for mankind is also a step upward for man. Our mechanical and scientific achievements can be called progress only in so far as they contribute to the well-being of mankind. As human values take precedence over material ones, man advances. All progress is progress towards the liberation and enrichment of human life, the recognition of the dignity and worth of every human soul. Phillips Brooks once said that every other element in authentic preaching completes itself in this, "that year by year the minister sees more deeply how well worthy of infinitely more than he can do for it is the human soul for which he works." [22] A world such as ours, in which millions are underfed and other millions starve, and yet others are displaced and driven about as though they were cattle, is a world that is sick unto death. The final test for the character of a nation or an age is the condition of its people. Human values are definitive.

So too Jesus' insight concerning the family of God. Our opposition to this concept of community is deep and far-reaching. Our own egoism resents it; our racial pride spurns it; our privileged position shuns it; our nationalistic pretensions and jeal-

---

[21] Quoted by Halford E. Luccock, *Preaching Values in the Old Testament in the Modern Translations*, p. 196.

[22] Quoted by W. A. Cameron, *Rainbows Through the Rain*, p. vii.

ousies fear it. But is it not now becoming evident that in opposing it we are kicking against the goads, going against the grain of the universe, and that if, due to incredible stupidity, we should continue, we may be signing our death warrant, even digging our own graves? For we are all members of God's family. This is the truth about life. We shall either learn to live together or we shall not live at all.

Or again, see how inescapable is his emphasis on inwardness. How this age confirms the truth that all real changes are changes from within out and not from the outside in. External changes as a rule no more alter the basic stuff of life than does changing a man's suit alter his character. Jesus taught that men had to be born again. This transformation is inner. It comes not from the outside in but inside out. It is the work of God within the soul. In preaching the Kingdom of God he was announcing the coming of a new age: "Behold, I make all things new." (Rev. 21:5.) But only new men can bring a new world. Only as men are made new creatures in Christ Jesus can they become creators of the new age. That truth this day declares.

> You cannot work the Utopian plan
> Until you find the Utopian man.[23]

If only we could get a new world by new plans, new schemes, new programs, we should long since have had it. But we cannot. Only a new man can build a new world.

Once we thought that science would give us a new world. This was the superstition we inherited from the nineteenth-

[23] Quoted by Lynn Harold Hough, *The Christian Criticism of Life*, p. 124.

century optimists, who seemed to believe that as the light of scientific knowledge entered our heads the darkness of sin would be driven from our hearts. They were mistaken. So are we. Science has given us a different world but in no sense is it new. Indeed Winston Churchill has warned about the Stone Age returning on the gleaming wings of science. If it does, however, it will not be the fault of science, which is wholly neutral, but of man. When shall we learn that it is not science which determines what man will do but man who decides what science does?

We thought that politics would give us a new world, that what the League of Nations did not do the United Nations would surely accomplish. But the United Nations, like the League, is at best only a tool, and while we cannot build a new house any more than a new world without tools, if we have nothing but tools we shall build neither. If the United Nations works men will make it work, and if it does not work men will keep it from working.

Again, we thought that economics would give us a new world. Karl Marx believed that could we but dethrone the capitalist and enthrone the proletariat, the equivalent of the Kingdom of God would come. Communism gives us a different world, but it is not new. Communism perhaps has some commendable insights but as it operates by and large in the world today there is nothing new about it. It is as new as arrogance, stubbornness, stupidity, and greed. Communism is as new as brutality, treachery, and tyranny. Communism, in short, is as new as human sin—and there is nothing new about that.

You will observe, then, how realistic Christianity is. It insists that man has to rebuild himself, or rather that God has to rebuild him, before he can rebuild the world. Until man is re-created nothing that he creates holds promise of his salvation.

We have said that Christ the Truth is truth in a life, that he is the truth about life. These observations life itself substantiates. But surely we cannot stop there. For if he is truth in a life and truth about life, it follows that he is truth about God, the Author and Sustainer of life. This is the supreme claim of the Christian faith. Though God has spoken to other men in other days, in Christ he has given his fullest, and many might say his final, revelation to man. This is the Christian faith.

This faith takes us beyond the boundaries of time, beyond our nicely calculated yes and no. It takes us even beyond the cross, where a man who had lived the life divine met a wholly unmerited death. For were we to stop there, with a cross, we should be, as Paul says, "of all men most miserable" (I Cor. 15:19). "If Christ be not risen, then is our preaching vain, and your faith is also vain" (I Cor. 15:14)—vain because even though his ethical insights would still be true, as they would be, the whole structure of his teaching would rest on a great illusion. Either Jesus conquered death or "his life is just an exquisite but pathetic absurdity." [24] It would be this because he would have been mistaken in the great premise from which he started.

That premise was that the universe is in the hands of a heavenly Father whose love far exceeds the love of a man for his children. But a universe whose final word to a life like

[24] William Pierce Merrill, *New York Times,* April 22, 1935.

Christ's is Golgotha, the place of skull, would be a universe without sense and surely without heart. It would be, in short, a universe without God. In such a universe preaching the gospel of God would indeed be vain. To his life and death on the cross, therefore, the Christian faith adds his resurrection. This is the crowning manifestation of Christ the Truth. It is because of this that "his image is sunny and still and strong with discovered life and comforting, like the wide dawn of an eternal Easter." [25]

For it is, as Paul says, his resurrection and nothing else, that declares him to be "the Son of God with power" (Rom. 1:4). But for this we should not be able to speak of him as our Saviour. Man's two great enemies are sin and death, and one who was himself vanquished by them could never offer to make his followers victors in their encounter. Whether we think of the Resurrection in terms of a physical body and empty tomb, as do the gospel writers, or think of the risen Christ as a spiritual Presence who meets us on the highways of the world, lives in us, and from whom nought can separate us, as does Paul, the fact is that without the Resurrection there could be no gospel—since without it there would have been no church. For the church was not founded to bear witness to a wise and good man done to death at the hands of cruel men. It was no monument to perpetuate the memory of some fallen hero. It was, as it is, a witness to the continuing presence and power of the living Christ, who, through his triumph over sin and death, offers abundant life to all the sons of men. The

[25] Hartley Burr Alexander, *Truth and the Faith*, p. 310.

Christian church, from the days of the apostles till now, has continued to bear witness to the reality of that claim. "His name through faith in his name hath made this man strong, whom ye see and know." (Acts 3:16.) From the days of the apostles until now Christ has been a life-giver. In Christ men through faith are brought in touch with the living God, experience his forgiving love, redeeming grace, and saving power. The testimony of Paul is still the faith of the church, "to wit, that God was in Christ, reconciling the world unto himself" (II Cor. 5:19).

This is the supreme truth about Christ. He is not only a prophet, though admittedly the greatest, nor a teacher, though surely the wisest, but a Saviour, the revelation of the living God. Through his life, death, and resurrection he makes real and operative God's redemptive grace. Thus he is able "to save . . . to the uttermost" (Heb. 7:25) those who come to God by him.

It is as the truth about God therefore that the church has found the consummation of Christ's life and teaching. This is the hub to which all his teachings point and from which, when securely anchored, they radiate. Why is the supreme truth a life rather than a law? Because in personality God speaks more clearly and convincingly to man than through any other medium. Why is the basic fact of life spiritual rather than material? Because "God is a Spirit" (John 4:24). Why the supreme worth and dignity of the individual? Because the individual is a child of God. Why is fellowship, community, the road to life? Because God is our heavenly Father and we are all members of his family. Why inner motive rather than out-

218

ward act? Because the Father "seeth in secret" (Matt. 6:4). It is because such insights are grounded in God and reveal his will for man that Jesus is the truth. Even as the sunlight reveals the true nature of the sun, so does Christ, who is "the brightness of his glory" (Heb. 1:3), reveal the true nature of God. But Christ could not have revealed this nature if death had marked the end of his matchless ministry. If he who lived the love of God had himself become the hapless victim of human treachery and sin, his teaching would indeed have been in vain. It is his triumph over sin and death that assures us his insights are not the hallucinations of a sincere but misguided mind but are of the very stuff of Reality itself—a revelation of the will and purpose of God.

And Pilate asked: "What is truth?" Ah, Pilate, had you but known! Your answer was there before you: truth in a life, truth about life, because the truth about him who is the Creator, Sustainer, Redeemer of life, of all things visible and invisible; who is above all yet in all, the God of truth from everlasting to everlasting, whose years shall have no end—God blessed forever.